Expert Defence

Raymond Brock

B. T. Batsford Ltd, *London*

First published 1997

© Raymond Brock 1997

ISBN 0 1734 8016 5

Typeset by Apsbridge Services Ltd, Nottingham
Printed by Redwood Books, Trowbridge, Wiltshire
for the publishers,
B. T. Batsford Ltd, 583 Fulham Road,
London SW6 5BY

A BATSFORD BRIDGE BOOK
Series Editor: Tony Sowter

CONTENTS

INTRODUCTION

As we said in *Step-by-Step: Planning the Defence*, we play bridge for a variety of reasons. Undoubtedly it gives us pleasure, but that pleasure comes from a number of different aspects – from winning, delight in a wondrous bidding sequence, brilliant play or a magical defence, or simply just from throwing cards around at a social occasion with little care for the outcome. But in truth, we all like to do the best we can.

Game All. Dealer West.

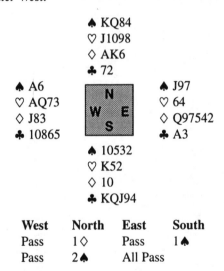

```
              ♠ KQ84
              ♡ J1098
              ◇ AK6
              ♣ 72
  ♠ A6          N          ♠ J97
  ♡ AQ73                    ♡ 64
  ◇ J83      W     E        ◇ Q97542
  ♣ 10865       S           ♣ A3
              ♠ 10532
              ♡ K52
              ◇ 10
              ♣ KQJ94
```

West	North	East	South
Pass	1◇	Pass	1♠
Pass	2♠	All Pass	

The Estonian pair of Viigand and Kase combined well to produce top defence against this two spade contract in the 1993 European Pairs. West led the eight of clubs to his partner's ace. Now came a heart switch and the defenders took two hearts and a heart ruff. East exited with a club. Declarer won and played a trump but West went in with the ace and played a fourth heart to allow East to make his jack of spades.

The beauty of the above hand is that East-West, having chosen a club lead, did little more than follow suit to get their good result – though West did have to go in with the first spade. However, that should not detract from the pleasure of having defended accurately.

We should take note of the words of that outstanding coach and captain Paul Stern (who developed the Vienna system and forced all his team to play it) whose strategy and tactical abilities led to the downfall of Ely Culbertson's team in 1937 at the hands of the Austrian sextet. After the Anschluss he made his home in Britain as did other notable Austrians, among them Fritzi Gordon and Rixi Markus. 'To win an International,' he would state, 'you do not need four bridge-players; you need four oxen who can sit and sit and push out the cards, so long as they are not horse-cards. If they do not go mad, they are sure to win.' Sound advice, although try convincing the juniors of that!

In truth, the bridge world now is not as straightforward a place as it was then and a little learning, or at least some good experience, is necessary.

Try your hand at the following problem:

Love All. Dealer East.

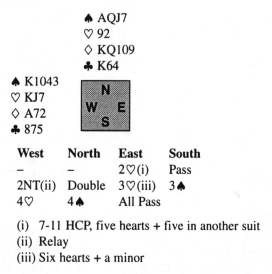

```
              ♠ AQJ7
              ♡ 92
              ◇ KQ109
              ♣ K64
  ♠ K1043
  ♡ KJ7        N
  ◇ A72      W   E
  ♣ 875        S
```

West	North	East	South
–	–	2♡(i)	Pass
2NT(ii)	Double	3♡(iii)	3♠
4♡	4♠	All Pass	

(i)   7-11 HCP, five hearts + five in another suit
(ii) Relay
(iii) Six hearts + a minor

You lead the king of hearts, followed by the jack of hearts, both of which hold, partner confirming he has a six-card suit. Plan the defence.

Gather the evidence: Partner has the ace-queen of hearts, so declarer must have the ace of clubs for his free bid. Apart from the ace of diamonds, there is little prospect of any further trick outside the trump suit.

Make a plan: Any experienced player will tell you that when the trump suit is less than solid, the best way to put declarer under pressure is to give a ruff and discard.

Implement the plan: Play the seven of hearts. The full deal:

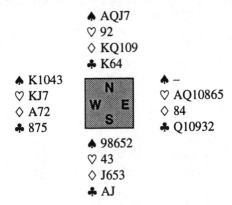

```
              ♠ AQJ7
              ♡ 92
              ◇ KQ109
              ♣ K64
    ♠ K1043                    ♠ -
    ♡ KJ7                      ♡ AQ10865
    ◇ A72                      ◇ 84
    ♣ 875                      ♣ Q10932
              ♠ 98652
              ♡ 43
              ◇ J653
              ♣ AJ
```

Declarer ruffed in hand, which was right, but pitched a low club from dummy which was not. Declarer now played a trump to the jack, which held, and then played high diamonds. West won the third round and exited with the eight of clubs to the queen and ace. Declarer was now an entry short to pick up the trumps and had to go one down.

After the jack of spades had held he could still have made his contract by cashing the king and ace of clubs and playing the nine of spades, covered by the ten and queen. Now he plays high diamonds. When West wins the third round and exits with a club, South can ruff with the eight in hand and take a further trump finesse for his contract.

The lesson to be learnt from this hand is that even when you know a contract is cold, try to make life as difficult as possible for declarer who may still go wrong.

It is often said that defence is the hardest part of the game. It is described thus because we have to ensure that partner is attuned to our intentions and we must seek to get the best out of him by improving our partnership co-operation and confidence. Having said that, sometimes there is an opportunity for a solo effort such as when we hold all the defensive cards. When there appears to be no hope of defeating a contract we have to use flair and imagination to create a situation where declarer will find a way to go down. If we paint the picture carefully, declarer may have some suspicions, particularly if our reputation precedes us, but is still likely to be led astray.

When you can defend as well as on the hand below you can truly call yourself one of the great players of the world.

Game All. Dealer South.

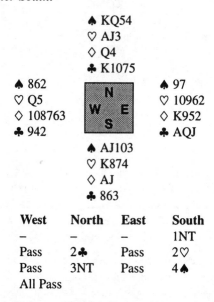

```
                    ♠ KQ54
                    ♡ AJ3
                    ◇ Q4
                    ♣ K1075
    ♠ 862                          ♠ 97
    ♡ Q5           N               ♡ 10962
    ◇ 108763    W     E            ◇ K952
    ♣ 942          S               ♣ AQJ
                    ♠ AJ103
                    ♡ K874
                    ◇ AJ
                    ♣ 863
```

West	North	East	South
–	–	–	1NT
Pass	2♣	Pass	2♡
Pass	3NT	Pass	4♠
All Pass			

East was the Brazilian star, Gabriel Chagas. His partner, Marcelo Branco, led the two of clubs, playing third and fifth highest leads. Even looking at all four hands it is hard to see a way for declarer to go down with both red-suit finesses working. However ... Chagas knew South's distribution because the opening lead showed he had three clubs and he already knew about four cards in both majors. He also knew that, even if West held the jack of diamonds, it would not help because declarer could eventually set up a club for a diamond discard. So...

Chagas won the jack of clubs, cashed the ace of clubs and switched to the nine of diamonds. Put yourself in declarer's position. He did not want to run the diamond and then lose a club ruff and it looked as if he could guarantee his contract by rising with the ace of diamonds and later finessing the ten of clubs, so establishing a parking place for the diamond loser. So that is precisely what he did. And, of course, Chagas won the queen of clubs and cashed the king of diamonds for one down. (I know that, for declarer's line to succeed, Branco must have led a falsecard at trick one, but that's not unheard of and it doesn't detract from Chagas's brilliance.)

Although as defenders, like declarer, we can see two hands, we cannot, as he can, determine our combined holding; we have to make assumptions that must be consistent with the information gathered about the hand from our own cards, the bidding, the dummy, declarer's line of play and partner's signals. From these assumptions we must develop a defence that keeps all options open, we must not panic and we must keep the defence fluid.

In this book there are further illustrations of the steps in defence – gathering the evidence, making a plan and implementing the plan – but we will introduce some new topics – influencing the defence during the bidding, partnership agreements, expert techniques, creating losing options and a master class – a whole chapter devoted to defences anyone would like to call their own.

And yet a word of caution … Many books on defence, or on declarer play for that matter, present us with problems where there is a clearcut reason for finding the correct defence at a particular moment in the play. In reality, even expert defenders do not know exactly what is going on all the time. But what expert defenders do when they do not know what is going on is avoid or postpone making a critical decision if at all possible. There are many no-cost plays to be found if we look for them. We have all seen defenders try one suit after another in a vain attempt to cash sufficient top tricks to beat a contract; one expert is often quoted as saying that every switch to a new suit in defence costs half a trick – had the defenders concentrated on keeping all their options open declarer would have had to struggle to find his own tricks.

Thus we see that although a good player may have only the outline of a plan prior to the lead he knows it is important to get off to a good start. The major decision is whether to be active or passive. The opponents' bidding may help us decide but generally we should be passive (i.e. non-committal) until there is enough evidence to decide on a satisfactory defence.

It follows that the best advice to give to an improving player is to defend passively more often than he does now. There are many hands where we cannot form a plan that will lead to the defeat of the contract but merely get off to the best start so that the sight of dummy and partner's signals will help extend the plan. This is particularly true of partscores.

Bridge is a game of mistakes; even the expert makes them but he says 'he took the wrong view'. Seriously though, the expert makes fewer mistakes than other players, that is the main secret of his success, not the brilliant coups that make the headlines. In addition, the expert is able to capitalise on his opponents' errors and that we must also do. That being the case, declarer in this book does not always play the hand to best advantage but that is no excuse for letting him make his contract.

On average we defend fifty per cent of the time, so any improvement that we can make in our defensive play is likely to produce significant benefits. Let us be defenders who make life difficult for declarer, for example, by routinely ducking an ace over a king-queen so that declarer will get a false picture of where the cards are or may waste an entry to lead up to the honour again. Such tactics will win many more points than any number of Merrimac or Crocodile Coups.

-0-0-0-0-0-0-

Finally, a word about our system and leading methods.

System

Unless marked to the contrary, please assume throughout the book that both partnerships are playing what has become a standard British system: weak (12-14) no trump, four-card majors (the higher ranking of two four-card suits is opened unless both majors, when one heart would be normal), Acol two bids. Where different methods are used, this will be announced accordingly.

Leads, signals and discards

In order for any of the following chapters to be meaningful, we must have an agreement as to our style of leads, signals and discards. There are many different styles in common use at tournament level and they all have their adherents and no doubt all have their good and not so good points. In this book some of the deals are presented as they occurred and then whatever method was used at the table is left unchanged; however, many deals are presented as problems and for those we must have a common system of carding.

Opening leads

Honour leads

In principle against no trumps we lead the top of honour sequences but there are several exceptions. The 'king' and 'ten' leads show a strong holding. The king asks partner to unblock (if possible) and otherwise give count, we might lead the king from KQ109x. It follows that if we decide to lead from KQ102 we cannot choose the king for fear of partner overtaking and perhaps eventually establishing a trick for declarer. What do we lead? The answer is the queen, and from the holding above we would not want partner to give us count but rather to encourage/ discourage. Furthermore, if the ten is to be a strong lead then we must not lead it from a holding such as 1098. Instead we choose to lead the nine.

Our leads against a suit contract are almost identical to the ones above, the one exception being that the ten is the normal top of a sequence or from an interior sequence. This style of leading provides an answer to the age-old problem of what to lead from ace-king. The answer is: it depends. On the ace partner will signal attitude so if we lead an unsupported ace against a high-level contract he can encourage if he holds the king. Alternatively we can lead the king from ace-king to obtain count and discover whether both tricks are cashing against a slam.

Small cards

Fourth highest from honours, second highest from small cards (including MUD).

Signals and discards

The first priority is to show distribution in the normal manner (i.e. high-low shows an even number). When attitude is given, a high card encourages. Secondary carding is suit preference (i.e. from 753 first play the 3 to show an odd number, then choose between the 7 and 5 according to suit preference).

When it is clear that length is not important, signals and discards may be attitude or suit preference. Some situations when this applies are:

(a) against a suit contract when there is a singleton in dummy, suit preference is given; also when it is known that declarer has a singleton.

(b) when a lead has set up a large number of tricks in dummy suit preference is given.

(c) when partner may have led a singleton, suit preference is given.

(d) where there is clearly some urgency to cash winners and only one discard is available, a high card would ask partner to play that suit.

(e) some other rare situations, e.g. unusual card selection on lead (suit preference, or even attitude).

1
THE STRATEGY OF DEFENCE

We will begin by recapping from *Step-by-Step: Planning the Defence*.

There we saw that there are certain steps that we should go through on every hand, whether it be slam, game or partscore, in no trumps or a suit contract, whether it is our lead or partner's. In later chapters we will look at some specific situations, but this chapter is concerned with good advice which can be applied to every hand.

On every hand we defend we should go through three steps when we are planning the defence:

Gather the evidence

Make a plan

Implement the plan

Whether you are an average player, beginner or expert, you should go through these steps. Many points can be lost by not making the maximum number of tricks so now we will not be content to defeat a contract but rather we will strive for the most that can be achieved with little risk.

Let us look now at some examples to reinforce the ideas.

Gather the evidence

The evidence is to be found in several areas:

1. The opponents' bidding
2. Our bidding (or lack of it)
3. The strength and distribution of our own hand
4. The sight of dummy
5. Partner's signals
6. Counting
7. Observing declarer's line of play

1. The opponents' bidding

   (a) *their general strength – are they minimum or maximum?*

   (b) *their distribution – the extent to which their bidding gives this away varies tremendously*

   (c) *their weak spots and their strong spots*

Love All. Dealer North.

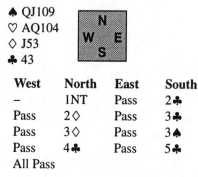

♠ QJ109
♡ AQ104
◇ J53
♣ 43

West	North	East	South
–	1NT	Pass	2♣
Pass	2◇	Pass	3♣
Pass	3◇	Pass	3♠
Pass	4♣	Pass	5♣
All Pass			

Gather the evidence: North/South have landed in five of a minor which is often a good sign for their opponents – if they are not a trick too high you can hope that they have missed a slam! This time they do not sound as if they have much extra strength.

Make a plan: Normally, when the opponents seem to be limited, it is a good time to make a passive lead and our spade holding is extremely suitable. This time, however, there is another consideration: it sounds as if they do not have a heart stopper or they would have tried to play in three no trumps.

Implement the plan: Lead the ace of hearts. The full deal:

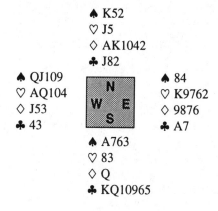

♠ K52
♡ J5
◇ AK1042
♣ J82

♠ QJ109
♡ AQ104
◇ J53
♣ 43

♠ 84
♡ K9762
◇ 9876
♣ A7

♠ A763
♡ 83
◇ Q
♣ KQ10965

The lead ensured that you cashed your two heart tricks to go with the ace of trumps to defeat the contract. On a spade lead declarer would win in hand, cash the queen of diamonds, cross to the king of spades, cash the ace and king of diamonds discarding hearts and concede a spade. He would later ruff a spade in the dummy and lose only a spade and a trump.

2. Our bidding (or lack of it)

There are a number of ways in which we can choose our bids in order to give partner (and the opponents) more information and so help him find the best defence.

Game All. Dealer East.

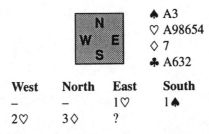

♠ A3
♡ A98654
◇ 7
♣ A632

West	North	East	South
–	–	1♡	1♠
2♡	3◇	?	

Your distribution and good controls clearly warrant a bid of four hearts. However, it is quite likely that this will provoke the opponents into bidding four spades. If they are going to bid four spades, it is important that your defence of that contract should start here. What can you bid to help partner with his opening lead? If partner holds as little as the king of hearts, you can see that you will probably be able to defeat four spades if you can score a diamond ruff to go along with your black-suit aces and one heart trick. Bid four diamonds.

Reese, in his excellent book *Develop Your Bidding Judgment*, made this suggestion over thirty years ago. Such bids have, for experienced partnerships, become standard practice these days.

3. The strength and distribution of our own hand

This will often tell us whether to be active or passive. Sometimes it is best to take our tricks, whilst on other occasions we do better to let the opponents make all the running. Most players enjoy being active and it goes against the grain to sit back and let declarer make his own mistakes. One sees this type of situation time and time again.

Game All. Dealer South.

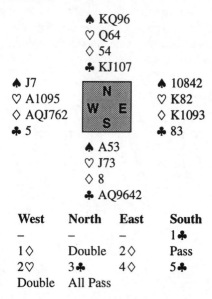

	♠ KQ96	
	♡ Q64	
	◇ 54	
	♣ KJ107	

♠ J7		♠ 10842
♡ A1095		♡ K82
◇ AQJ762		◇ K1093
♣ 5		♣ 83

	♠ A53	
	♡ J73	
	◇ 8	
	♣ AQ9642	

West	North	East	South
–	–	–	1♣
1◇	Double	2◇	Pass
2♡	3♣	4◇	5♣
Double	All Pass		

West leads the ace of diamonds against South's doubled game. East plays the ten suggesting a four-card holding. West now tries the ace of hearts and, in response to East's encouraging eight, continues with a second heart. Declarer soon claims the remainder and East/West score 200.

What was the hurry? Suppose West had continued with a second diamond at trick two. Declarer would have ruffed, drawn trumps, tried spades, and eventually had to concede three heart tricks. East/West would have scored 500, a significant improvement.

Assuming declarer has six clubs (with seven he would probably have bid over two diamonds; with five he would probably have passed four diamonds), the only time an immediate heart switch gains a trick is when declarer has ♠A10x and ♡xxx. This is against the odds since East, with four small spades to South's two, is twice as likely to hold the ten. In addition, with hearts as good as KJx, East should have played the king of diamonds at trick one.

On the other hand, sometimes it is essential to be active. This doesn't only mean hurriedly cashing tricks; it can also include such areas as attacking declarer's entries or cutting his communications.

Love All. Dealer North.

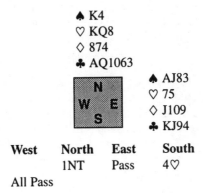

```
              ♠ K4
              ♡ KQ8
              ◇ 874
              ♣ AQ1063
                            ♠ AJ83
                 N          ♡ 75
              W     E       ◇ J109
                 S          ♣ KJ94
```

West	North	East	South
	1NT	Pass	4♡
All Pass			

Your partner leads the six of spades to your jack which holds, declarer playing the five. You cash the ace of spades, declarer playing the nine and partner the two. Plan the defence.

Gather the evidence: It looks as if partner has led from ♠Q10762. You may have more defensive tricks in clubs but that will depend on declarer's length in the suit. Partner may have a trick or two in diamonds.

Make a plan: It looks natural to play a diamond, hoping to take whatever tricks partner has in the suit. However, your club holding is so good that you know that any tricks partner has in diamonds cannot go anywhere for a while. The danger is that declarer may have a singleton club and be able to set up a long club trick for a diamond discard. The best way to prevent him from doing this is to take out one of dummy's trump entries prematurely.

Implement the plan: Play a trump. The full deal:

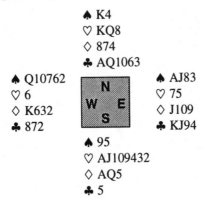

```
                    ♠ K4
                    ♡ KQ8
                    ◇ 874
                    ♣ AQ1063
     ♠ Q10762                        ♠ AJ83
     ♡ 6              N              ♡ 75
     ◇ K632        W     E          ◇ J109
     ♣ 872            S              ♣ KJ94
                    ♠ 95
                    ♡ AJ109432
                    ◇ AQ5
                    ♣ 5
```

Declarer can win the trump in hand, play a club to the ace and ruff a club. He can play a trump back to dummy and ruff another club, but now he has only one trump left in dummy. If he crosses to dummy and ruffs another club he has no entry to reach the established trick there. He will undoubtedly take a diamond finesse and go down.

Suppose, instead, that you had returned the jack of diamonds at trick three. Declarer would be in no hurry to take the finesse. He would rise with the ace of diamonds and play a club to the ace and ruff a club. Now he would play a heart to the king and ruff a club, a heart to the queen and ruff a club. He can then cross back to dummy's eight of hearts (he will surely have ruffed clubs high in his hand when necessary) and cash the fifth club discarding a diamond.

4. The sight of dummy

Game All. Dealer South.

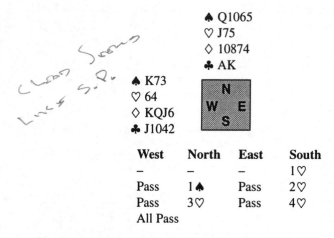

♠ Q1065
♡ J75
◇ 10874
♣ AK

♠ K73
♡ 64
◇ KQJ6
♣ J1042

West	North	East	South
–	–	–	1♡
Pass	1♠	Pass	2♡
Pass	3♡	Pass	4♡
All Pass			

You lead the king of diamonds against South's four hearts. Partner plays the two and declarer the three. You continue with the queen of diamonds, partner playing the five and declarer the nine. Plan the rest of the defence.

Gather the evidence: You have two defensive tricks in diamonds and probably one in spades. You may make a trump – perhaps partner has the ace – or a second spade if partner has either the ace or the jack and declarer misguesses.

Make a plan: It is important for you to know whether or not to go in with your king of spades when declarer leads towards dummy's holding. If declarer has a doubleton spade you will need to go in with your king, otherwise he will not lose a spade. Ducking the spade will let him make an unnecessary trick, either his tenth or eleventh depending or whether partner has a trump trick. If declarer has a trebleton spade you need to duck your king and hope he goes wrong. His bidding suggests a six-card heart suit. If you can find out how many clubs he has you will be able to work out what to do in spades.

Implement the plan: Play the two of clubs. Partner plays the three. You assume he has five clubs and declarer a doubleton (otherwise declarer's distribution is 1-6-2-4 and you have no hope of beating the contract). That leaves declarer with three spades. When he ruffs a diamond to hand and leads a low spade you know to play small nonchalantly and he may guess wrong. The full deal:

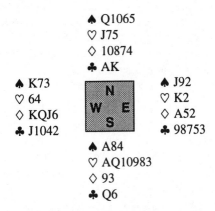

            ♠ Q1065
            ♡ J75
            ◊ 10874
            ♣ AK

♠ K73   ♠ J92
♡ 64   ♡ K2
◊ KQJ6   ◊ A52
♣ J1042   ♣ 98753

            ♠ A84
            ♡ AQ10983
            ◊ 93
            ♣ Q6

Had partner played a high club you would have worked out that declarer had a doubleton spade. Now you must go in with your king of spades in case declarer has ♠A4 ♡KQ10983 ◊93 ♣Q63. Note that declarer has done well to play spades before trumps so you cannot know whether partner has a trump trick.

The sight of dummy here caused us to extend our plan: we needed to acquire information in order to know what to do when declarer came to make his critical 'guess'. We got this information from partner's signal. There are many other examples of partner's signals that assist us to plan a good defence.

5. Partner's signals

Game All. Dealer East.

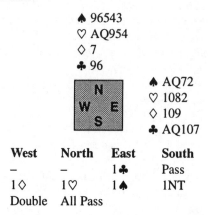

```
                    ♠ 96543
                    ♡ AQ954
                    ◊ 7
                    ♣ 96
                                      ♠ AQ72
                                      ♡ 1082
                                      ◊ 109
                                      ♣ AQ107
```

West	North	East	South
–	–	1♣	Pass
1◊	1♡	1♠	1NT
Double	All Pass		

Your partner leads the two of clubs against South's one no trump. You win with the ace and switch to the ten of diamonds. When this holds you continue with the nine of diamonds which also holds, dummy discarding a spade. You now return the ten of clubs (in case partner started with K82) to declarer's jack and partner's king and he continues with the king of diamonds. Dummy discards another low spade. What do you throw?

Gather the evidence: Dummy has made a very aggressive vulnerable overcall, presumably hoping to help his partner with the opening lead. It will probably not be enough simply to beat one no trump, rather you may need to beat it by sufficient to compensate for your game. It looks as if partner started with ◊ KQJxx and ♣Kxx. That may be all he has, in which case declarer will make his contract. It is likely that declarer has the king of spades (he did bid one no trump over your one spade) but partner may have the king of hearts, in which case declarer may not make many tricks at all.

Make a plan: The problem is that partner does not have an obvious entry to his established diamonds. Furthermore, you are under some pressure here. You cannot discard a heart for fear that declarer's jack will pin your ten; you do not want to discard a club as that may make it easy for declarer to establish a trick in the suit. So it looks as if you should throw a spade.

Execute the plan: Your best hope to create an entry to your partner's hand is to play him for ♠Jx (a holding he has suggested by his play of the king of diamonds), in which case you need to discard your spade queen. The full deal:

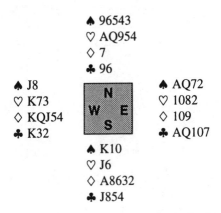

```
                    ♠ 96543
                    ♡ AQ954
                    ◊ 7
                    ♣ 96
        ♠ J8          N          ♠ AQ72
        ♡ K73                     ♡ 1082
        ◊ KQJ54    W     E        ◊ 109
        ♣ K32         S           ♣ AQ107
                    ♠ K10
                    ♡ J6
                    ◊ A8632
                    ♣ J854
```

Declarer wins the ace of diamonds and plays the jack of hearts to the king and ace. What can he do? His best chance of making a reasonable number of tricks is to play a spade to his king and heart to dummy's nine but that will be disastrous for him here. He can never make more than four tricks.

Now let us suppose that you discarded a low spade. Declarer wins the ace of diamonds, takes a heart finesse and plays a spade. Over to you. If you play the ace and exit with a spade he can win, cross to a heart and play a third spade and you will have to give him a club trick at the end; if you play a low spade he will win the king and exit with a spade and your best defence now is to give him a club trick straightaway; finally, if you put in the queen of spades he can duck and you will again be endplayed later on to give him a fifth trick.

It may not seem that this third undertrick is very important but many pairs will bid and make three no trumps with your cards. So at Pairs the difference between 500 and 800 is likely to be the difference between a top and a bottom; at Teams it is the difference between losing 3 IMPs and gaining 5, a total difference of 8 IMPs, well worth having.

6. **Counting**
    (a) counting points
    (b) counting distribution
    (c) counting tricks

East/West Game. Dealer East.

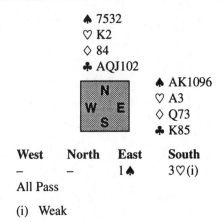

♠ 7532
♥ K2
♦ 84
♣ AQJ102

♠ AK1096
♥ A3
♦ Q73
♣ K85

West	North	East	South
–	–	1♠	3♥(i)
All Pass			

(i) Weak

Your partner leads the four of spades which you win with the king, declarer playing the jack. Plan the defence.

Gather the evidence: Presumably declarer has one spade and six hearts but his minor-suit distribution is unclear.

Make a plan: If declarer has two diamonds and four clubs it does not matter what you do now but if he has more than two diamonds you should be thinking about cutting down dummy's ruffing potential. The trouble is that if you play ace and another heart now he will simply draw trumps and take a club finesse; if he has the ace of diamonds he will make ten tricks. The solution is to keep control by playing a low trump.

Implement the plan: Play the three of hearts. The full deal:

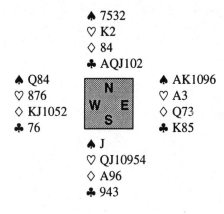

♠ 7532
♥ K2
♦ 84
♣ AQJ102

♠ Q84
♥ 876
♦ KJ1052
♣ 76

♠ AK1096
♥ A3
♦ Q73
♣ K85

♠ J
♥ QJ10954
♦ A96
♣ 943

On a low heart switch declarer has no chance. If he ducks a diamond you will cash the ace of hearts and continue with a diamond; if he plays another trump you will switch to a diamond; if he takes a club finesse you will duck and you may later be able to give your partner a club ruff. Whatever declarer chooses he is doomed.

7. Observing declarer's line of play

Love All. Dealer North.

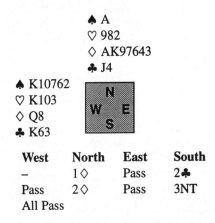

	♠ A
	♡ 982
	◊ AK97643
	♣ J4

♠ K10762
♡ K103
◊ Q8
♣ K63

West	North	East	South
–	1◊	Pass	2♣
Pass	2◊	Pass	3NT
All Pass			

You lead the six of spades against South's 3NT. Dummy's ace wins as partner plays the eight and declarer the four. At trick two declarer plays a low diamond from the dummy to partner's five, his ten and your queen. Plan the play.

Gather the evidence: Dummy looks rather threatening with six sure tricks to take as soon as he gets the lead. Of course, declarer's play can only be explained if he has precisely a doubleton diamond. So, do you need to take four top tricks immediately, before declarer takes nine? The answer to that is clearly no, because if that were the case declarer would have taken his only chance, that of a 2-2 diamond break.

Make a plan: In order for declarer's play to make sense he must have QJx of spades. In addition partner must have an ace or declarer has nine top tricks whatever you do. You could try to put partner in with his ace, say in hearts, and hope that he had sense to switch to the remaining suit, say clubs. This would beat the contract but there are lots of things that could go wrong. There is a much simpler idea: play a diamond back and make declarer take his winners immediately. This will surely squeeze his hand and make the later defence much easier.

Implement the plan: Play the eight of diamonds. The full deal:

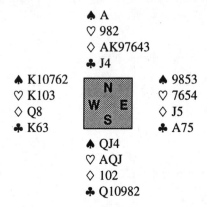

After cashing his diamonds everyone will be reduced to five cards and declarer's hand is hopelessly squeezed. His only chance is the heart finesse. He will probably come down to the queen-jack of spades, the ace-queen of hearts and a club. It should be a simple matter for you to keep the king of spades, king and another heart and king and another club. If he takes a heart finesse you can cash out; if he plays a club partner will win his ace and play a heart through declarer.

Make a plan

The various considerations to be taken into account when making a plan are:

1. Assume the contract can be defeated
2. Play partner for the minimum
3. Technique
4. Flexibility
5. Deception

1. Assume the contract can be defeated

In *Step-by-Step: Planning the Defence* it was considered sufficient to beat the contract, but it is expensive to keep forfeiting undertricks, especially if doubled or vulnerable. Expert defence aims for as many tricks as possible most of the time, only taking the safe option when to do otherwise would risk letting declarer make his contract. Only at Matchpointed Pairs can it be right to risk allowing a contract to make in order to save overtricks.

Game All. Dealer South.

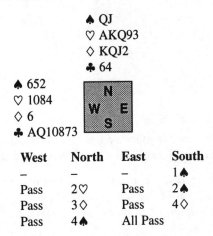

♠ QJ
♡ AKQ93
◇ KQJ2
♣ 64

♠ 652
♡ 1084
◇ 6
♣ AQ10873

West	North	East	South
–	–	–	1♠
Pass	2♡	Pass	2♠
Pass	3◇	Pass	4◇
Pass	4♠	All Pass	

You lead your singleton diamond against South's four spades. Partner wins with the ace and switches to the jack of clubs to the king and your ace. Plan the defence.

Gather the evidence: There is no use getting cross with partner for not giving you a diamond ruff. Maybe he could not tell that you had a singleton or, more likely since the bidding has been very revealing, maybe he has his own plan. Dummy is surprisingly strong for his bidding. You have already seen 32 HCP. Declarer must have the ace and king of spades.

Make a plan: It seems that the only chance of beating the contract is to put partner in and get a diamond ruff. You have already worked out that he will not be able to overruff dummy's queen of spades. You also know that spades are breaking for declarer so that it is not possible to promote a trump trick. The only chance seems to be to find partner with the nine of clubs.

Implement the plan: Play the three of clubs. The full deal:

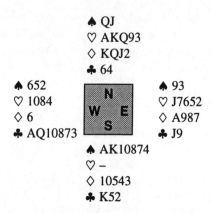

```
            ♠ QJ
            ♡ AKQ93
            ◇ KQJ2
            ♣ 64
♠ 652              ♠ 93
♡ 1084             ♡ J7652
◇ 6                ◇ A987
♣ AQ10873          ♣ J9
            ♠ AK10874
            ♡ –
            ◇ 10543
            ♣ K52
```

Partner has done very well. If he had given you a diamond ruff immediately the defence would have had no chance. All you could have done would have been to cash the ace of clubs to save the overtrick.

It is true that your defence might have presented declarer with an unnecessary overtrick if he had had the nine of clubs, but that was worth the risk. Note that returning a small club would also have worked if partner had had a singleton.

2.   Play partner for the minimum

If we need to guess, then we should play partner for the most likely minimum holding that he needs for us to beat the contract. However, we should not need to guess very often. There are usually pointers to help us work out partner's hand as we have seen under 'Gather the Evidence'.

Love All. Dealer West.

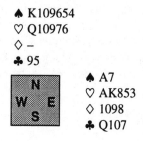

```
            ♠ K109654
            ♡ Q10976
            ◇ –
            ♣ 95
                   ♠ A7
                   ♡ AK853
                   ◇ 1098
                   ♣ Q107
```

West	North	East	South
1◊(i)	1♠	2♡	Pass
3♣	Pass	3NT	4◊
Double	All Pass		

(i) Either clubs, diamonds or a balanced hand

Your partner leads the jack of hearts to the queen and king. Plan the defence.

Gather the evidence: Your own hand is very suitable for defence and it is your partner who has doubled. While, of course, you must be certain you beat the contract, it is probably a case of trying to take the maximum penalty, especially if your game had been going to make. One immediate observation is that dummy appears to have no entry.

Make a plan: You know that declarer has at most a doubleton heart and surely would have bid earlier if he had more than a doubleton spade. Because he has no entry to dummy, you also need to avoid giving him a chance in clubs that he would not otherwise have. If partner has the ace and jack it will work out alright to play a club, but if he has only the ace a club switch will give declarer an unnecessary chance. Playing partner for a minimum, the safest line of defence is to play a second top heart.

Implement the plan: Play the king of hearts. The full deal:

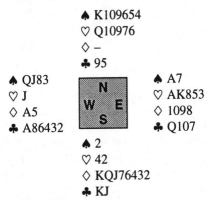

```
              ♠ K109654
              ♡ Q10976
              ◊ –
              ♣ 95
♠ QJ83                      ♠ A7
♡ J                         ♡ AK853
◊ A5          N             ◊ 1098
♣ A86432    W   E           ♣ Q107
                S
              ♠ 2
              ♡ 42
              ◊ KQJ76432
              ♣ KJ
```

If it is declarer who has the singleton heart, nothing is lost as you can prevent him getting to dummy. However, when declarer follows, partner can signal to help you defend. If he had the ace and jack of clubs he would surely discard a high club; on the actual hand the eight of spades would be more helpful. Now, as long as you don't play a club, it doesn't really matter. If you play a trump, partner can win and play the queen of spades and you will later come to two club tricks; you could play a third heart – no doubt declarer would discard a spade while partner ruffed. As the cards lie you will always take 500.

3. Technique

There are certain aspects of defence, as there are of declarer play, where the expert develops good habits of technique. For an expert defender there are many situations where he plays differently from the average player because of the experience he has gained over the years. He will regularly and smoothly duck declarer's honours, play certain false cards, unblock his honours, adopt an active or passive defensive role, know when to split honours, be thinking about how to break up a squeeze or endplay etc, etc.

Game All. Dealer South.

♠ 764
♡ 1064
◇ AKJ98
♣ 93

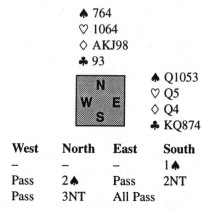

♠ Q1053
♡ Q5
◇ Q4
♣ KQ874

West	North	East	South
–	–	–	1♠
Pass	2♠	Pass	2NT
Pass	3NT	All Pass	

West leads the seven of hearts against three no trumps and your queen is won by declarer's king. Declarer now plays the five of diamonds to partner's seven and dummy's eight. Plan the defence.

Gather the evidence: Partner is playing high-low in diamonds. He must have four cards in the suit for with a nine-card fit, declarer would play at least one top honour first. The heart position is unclear: perhaps the seven is fourth highest in which case the suit might now be good, or it could be second highest from several small cards.

Make a plan: You could win the queen of diamonds and return a heart but what is the hurry? Declarer is not psychic. Provided you duck smoothly, will he not return to hand with a black-suit card and take another diamond finesse. You will then win your queen and return a heart. With no communications between the two hands declarer will surely lose as many tricks as it is possible for you to take.

Implement the plan: Play the four of diamonds. The full deal:

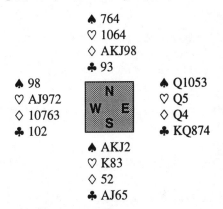

```
              ♠ 764
              ♡ 1064
              ◇ AKJ98
              ♣ 93
♠ 98                         ♠ Q1053
♡ AJ972                      ♡ Q5
◇ 10763                      ◇ Q4
♣ 102                        ♣ KQ874
              ♠ AKJ2
              ♡ K83
              ◇ 52
              ♣ AJ65
```

In the event partner's seven of hearts was fourth-best so you could have won the queen of diamonds and beaten the contract immediately. That would have led to one down. By ducking the diamond the contract went three down.

One of the most fundamental concepts in the play of the cards at bridge is 'communications'. Both sides try to preserve their own communications whilst trying to sever those of their opponents'.

Love All. Dealer North.

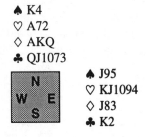

```
              ♠ K4
              ♡ A72
              ◇ AKQ
              ♣ QJ1073
                             ♠ J95
                             ♡ KJ1094
                             ◇ J83
                             ♣ K2
```

West	North	East	South
–	1♣	1♡	1♠
Pass	2♡	Pass	2NT
Pass	3NT	All Pass	

Your partner leads the six of hearts against South's three no trumps. Declarer plays dummy's two. Plan the defence.

Gather the evidence: It looks as if partner has a doubleton heart, leaving declarer with Qxx.

Make a plan: Dummy looks to have all the other suits sufficiently guarded so it is unlikely you will beat the contract outside the heart suit. If you win the king of hearts and return the suit you know you do not have enough entries both to establish and cash the suit.

Implement the plan: Play the nine of hearts. The full deal:

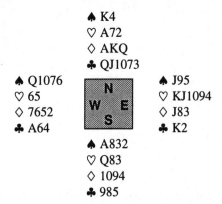

```
              ♠ K4
              ♡ A72
              ◇ AKQ
              ♣ QJ1073
  ♠ Q1076                    ♠ J95
  ♡ 65          N            ♡ KJ1094
  ◇ 7652     W     E         ◇ J83
  ♣ A64          S           ♣ K2
              ♠ A832
              ♡ Q83
              ◇ 1094
              ♣ 985
```

Declarer wins the queen of hearts and plays a club but West goes in with the ace and plays a second heart. When you get the lead with the king of clubs you can cash two more heart winners.

If declarer ducks the jack of hearts East must switch (a heart continuation would allow declarer to make his contract since West would not have a heart left to play when he won the ace of clubs); when West wins the first club a second heart will ensure two off.

4. Flexibility

Often there is not enough evidence to form any sort of scheme, let alone a formal plan so we must seek to get our side off to a good start and obtain the extra information we need. Thus we need to be passive and flexible.

Game All. Dealer West.

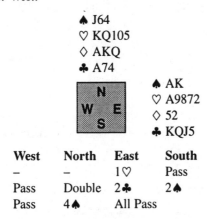

```
                    ♠ J64
                    ♡ KQ105
                    ◊ AKQ
                    ♣ A74
                                    ♠ AK
              N                     ♡ A9872
          W       E                 ◊ 52
              S                     ♣ KQJ5
```

West	North	East	South
–	–	1♡	Pass
Pass	Double	2♣	2♠
Pass	4♠	All Pass	

Your partner leads the four of hearts against four spades. Dummy plays the queen and you win with the ace as declarer plays the three. Plan the defence.

Gather the evidence: You can see three defensive tricks in the majors, but it is not clear whether the fourth will come from a club trick or giving partner a heart ruff – you know from the lead that partner has one or three hearts.

Make a plan: You need to form a plan that has the flexibility to cater for both possibilities. If you play a heart back and partner has three cards in the suit it could be a disaster. If, on the other hand, you return the king of clubs, partner will give you count in the suit, but when he plays low you will not know whether he has five clubs and one heart or three clubs and three hearts. However, if you return the *queen* of clubs he will tell you whether or not he likes the suit. It may seem that that information is of no use in this example, but if partner is thinking along the right lines he should know that you need to choose between hearts and clubs for extra defensive tricks. If he has a singleton heart he should discourage clubs whereas with heart length he should encourage.

Implement the plan: Play the queen of clubs. The full deal:

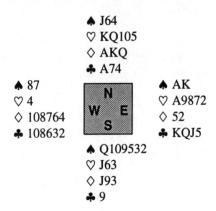

```
                    ♠ J64
                    ♡ KQ105
                    ◇ AKQ
                    ♣ A74
♠ 87                              ♠ AK
♡ 4                               ♡ A9872
◇ 108764                          ◇ 52
♣ 108632                          ♣ KQJ5
                    ♠ Q109532
                    ♡ J63
                    ◇ J93
                    ♣ 9
```

5. Deception

There is a whole new subject in deception, or rather creating losing options for declarer. Not every hand can be defeated; sometimes declarer must be persuaded to go down.

North/South Game. Dealer South.

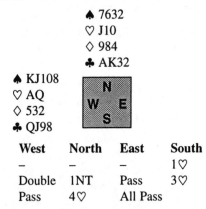

```
                    ♠ 7632
                    ♡ J10
                    ◇ 984
                    ♣ AK32
♠ KJ108
♡ AQ
◇ 532
♣ QJ98
```

West	North	East	South
–	–	–	1♡
Double	1NT	Pass	3♡
Pass	4♡	All Pass	

You lead the queen of clubs against South's four hearts. Dummy plays the king, partner the four and declarer the five. Declarer now plays the jack of hearts – five, two. Plan the defence.

Gather the evidence: Declarer probably has a seven-card heart suit as he has made a jump rebid missing so many high honours.

Make a plan: Dummy is extremely short of entries. You removed one of them at trick one. When you play another club declarer will be in dummy for the last time. If you win the queen of hearts he may use that entry to take a winning diamond finesse. How can you deflect him? If you win the *ace* of hearts, will he not use his one remaining entry to take the finesse he *knows* is winning, the heart finesse?

Implement the plan: Win the *ace* of hearts and play another club. The full deal:

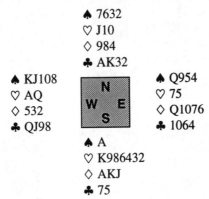

                    ♠ 7632
                    ♡ J10
                    ◇ 984
                    ♣ AK32
    ♠ KJ108   ♠ Q954
    ♡ AQ   ♡ 75
    ◇ 532   ◇ Q1076
    ♣ QJ98   ♣ 1064
                    ♠ A
                    ♡ K986432
                    ◇ AKJ
                    ♣ 75

Provided you did your thinking in a split second and did not give the game away with a pause, declarer is sure to go wrong. Put yourself in his shoes. Why take a finesse that *may* be right (and the bidding suggests isn't) instead of one that you *know* is right (and the bidding also reinforces that opinion).

Implement the plan

This should be the most straightforward aspect. We have decided what to do, now all we need is to do it. The most common mistake here is to fail to appreciate that partner might not know our plan. Sometimes we have to go out of our way to make sure that partner does not go wrong and sometimes we need some conventional agreements so that we can tell partner what it's all about.

Game All. Dealer South.

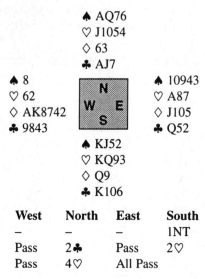

```
                    ♠ AQ76
                    ♡ J1054
                    ◊ 63
                    ♣ AJ7
  ♠ 8                              ♠ 10943
  ♡ 62              N              ♡ A87
  ◊ AK8742      W       E          ◊ J105
  ♣ 9843            S              ♣ Q52
                    ♠ KJ52
                    ♡ KQ93
                    ◊ Q9
                    ♣ K106
```

West	North	East	South
–	–	–	1NT
Pass	2♣	Pass	2♡
Pass	4♡	All Pass	

This deal occurred in a World Championship several years ago. West led the ace and king of diamonds and switched to the eight of spades. Declarer won in dummy and played the jack of hearts. Would you have been awake enough to rise with the ace and give partner a spade ruff? It was not so easy. There was nothing in the bidding to indicate that partner held a singleton spade and East might have looked pretty foolish if partner had had the doubleton (or even singleton) queen of hearts.

How much easier it would have been if East/West had been playing what is now a widely used leading convention whereby the lead of a *king* from ace-king followed by a switch sends a message to partner that the switch is a singleton.

So far there is only a little that is new. That is because even expert defenders go through the basic thought processes on every hand. However, in this book we are going to elaborate on a few more strategies of which we have already given at least one example.

2

BEFORE YOU SEE DUMMY

It is not completely clear when the defence starts. In *Step-by-Step: Planning the Defence*, we decided to start with the opening lead. In this book we are going to start even earlier as it is often possible to 'bid for the defence'.

As in any other area of card play we have the same three steps to go through:

Gather the evidence

Make a plan

Implement the plan

One of the main things to decide on every hand is whether to try to be active or passive. Sometimes it sounds as if the opponents have plenty of values, perhaps they have bid 1♠ – 3♣ – 3♠ – 4♠, or even 1♠ – 3♠ – 4♣ – 4♠. Unless it looks as we have some nasty surprises for them they are probably strong enough to make their contract if left to their own devices. This is the time to underlead an honour or perhaps try for a somewhat far-fetched ruff, i.e. be *active*.

On the other hand, if the bidding has gone 1♠ – 2♠ – 2NT – 3♠ – 4♠, they have probably stretched. Provided we don't give them a trick they may well go down, particularly if the cards do not lie too well for them. Whatever we do we don't want to give them a vital extra trick on the opening lead, i.e. we want to be *passive*.

We covered this topic in some depth in *Step-by-Step: Planning the Defence* and will not dwell on it here, but it is important to consider the appropriate approach on every single hand.

North/South Game. Dealer North

♠ 92
♡ 8742
◇ K10
♣ 109763

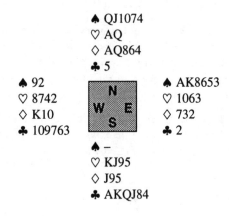

West	North	East	South
–	1♠	Pass	2♣
Pass	2◇	Pass	2♡
Pass	3◇	Pass	4♣
Pass	4♡	Pass	6♣
All Pass			

Gather the evidence: You expect declarer to hold what he thinks is a solid club suit since he has bid a slam without any support from his partner. You have a nasty surprise for him there. On the other hand, you probably have a very nice surprise for him in diamonds. Your partner has not doubled the four heart cue-bid so is unlikely to hold a useful holding in that suit.

Make a plan: It is very likely that your doubleton king of diamonds will enable declarer to play that suit for a number of tricks with no loss which is just what he will need to do when he finds that he has a trump loser. If you can force him to play diamonds before he knows that he has a trump loser he may well go wrong.

Implement the plan: Lead the ten of diamonds. The full deal:

```
                    ♠ QJ1074
                    ♡ AQ
                    ◇ AQ864
                    ♣ 5
      ♠ 92                          ♠ AK8653
      ♡ 8742          N             ♡ 1063
      ◇ K10        W     E          ◇ 732
      ♣ 109763        S             ♣ 2
                    ♠ –
                    ♡ KJ95
                    ◇ J95
                    ♣ AKQJ84
```

This hand occurred in the inaugural Senior European Teams Championship and was a triumph for the British quartet. The British declarer received a spade lead which he ruffed. He then drew four rounds of trumps and was able to take advantage of the favourable diamond position.

In the other room the British West, Roy Garthwaite, found the dynamic lead of the ten of diamonds. This looked too much like a singleton to declarer. He rose with the ace and the contract was doomed.

There is one further point of interest in the hand. On a non-diamond lead declarer will win, draw four rounds of trumps and play a diamond. West should play the king. On this hand it does not help as declarer needs only three diamond tricks, but on a different lay-out it may persuade him to play a diamond to the nine on the next round.

Game All. Dealer South.

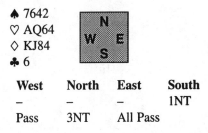

♠ 7642
♡ AQ64
◊ KJ84
♣ 6

West	North	East	South
–	–	–	1NT
Pass	3NT	All Pass	

It could obviously be right to lead any suit but even though North/South have shown unlimited values, it would be a pity to start off by giving them a trick so the passive six of spades looks the most attractive.

♠ AK5
♡ K83
◊ A765
♣ 543

♠ 7642
♡ AQ64
◊ KJ84
♣ 6

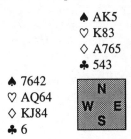

Declarer wins the ace of spades in dummy while partner plays the eight and declarer the three. He now leads a diamond to his ten. Plan the defence.

Gather the evidence: Dummy is fairly minimum for a jump to three no trumps. Although he has 14 HCP, the hand is very flat and short of intermediate cards. Partner has played the lowest outstanding spade, consistent with a three-card holding. Of course, he might not have played an honour from honour doubleton.

Make a plan: There seems to be no great rush to do anything here. Your holdings in the red suits look promising but you would rather it were declarer who broached the suits. All in all, it looks best to plod away with spades and let declarer make his own mistakes.

Implement the plan: Play the two of spades. The full deal:

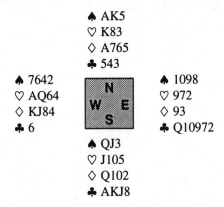

<pre>
                    ♠ AK5
                    ♡ K83
                    ◇ A765
                    ♣ 543
    ♠ 7642   ♠ 1098
    ♡ AQ64   N   ♡ 972
    ◇ KJ84   W   E   ◇ 93
    ♣ 6   S   ♣ Q10972
                    ♠ QJ3
                    ♡ J105
                    ◇ Q102
                    ♣ AKJ8
</pre>

No doubt declarer will win the second spade in dummy and play another diamond. You will win and clear the spades. Declarer can still make his contract by finessing you for the eight of diamonds and perhaps he will do this. More to the point, he might have done better to play on clubs before diamonds which would have put you to some awkward early discards. However, the main issue is that there was nothing you could do to help your side, only to help declarer. Your best defence was to persevere passively and hope declarer went wrong.

The tactics covered in this chapter will be considered under the following headings:

1. Suit preference
2. Trump leads
3. Be sensible
4. Conventions
5. Bidding for the defence

1. Suit preference

Usually suit-preference signals occur after the opening lead has been made but sometimes the lead itself can be a signal.

Sometimes we lead a suit-preference card in a long suit, typically when we have pre-empted, with a side void.

Game All. Dealer West.

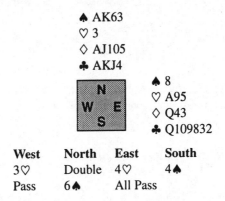

```
              ♠ AK63
              ♡ 3
              ◊ AJ105
              ♣ AKJ4
                              ♠ 8
                              ♡ A95
                              ◊ Q43
                              ♣ Q109832
```

West	North	East	South
3♡	Double	4♡	4♠
Pass	6♠	All Pass	

West leads the six of hearts against South's six spades. You play the ace which holds, South playing the two. Plan the defence.

Gather the evidence: Partner's opening lead is very strange. You would expect at least a very good six-card suit for a vulnerable three opener and yet he has not chosen to lead a top honour. Partner is likely to have three trumps on this sequence, yet he has chosen to lead his own suit so is unlikely to have a singleton in a side suit.

Make a plan: If you are right in your surmise that partner has three trumps, then he *must* have shortage in one of the side suits and yet he has not led a singleton. It looks as if he might well have a void and wants to make sure we win trick one, which is why he has not led a top honour in his suit. The six cannot be the highest spot card he has but it might well be the lowest.

Implement the plan: Play the three of clubs. The full deal:

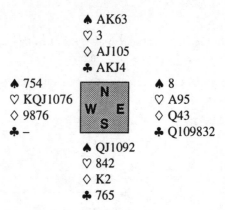

```
                  ♠ AK63
                  ♡ 3
                  ◇ AJ105
                  ♣ AKJ4
      ♠ 754                      ♠ 8
      ♡ KQJ1076      N           ♡ A95
      ◇ 9876       W   E         ◇ Q43
      ♣ −            S           ♣ Q109832
                  ♠ QJ1092
                  ♡ 842
                  ◇ K2
                  ♣ 765
```

Partner ruffs your club to defeat the slam. Had you returned anything else declarer would surely have played you for the queen of diamonds and made his slam.

Recently some good players have extended this thought by introducing suit preference into trump leads.

Game All. Dealer South.

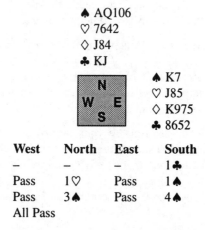

```
                  ♠ AQ106
                  ♡ 7642
                  ◇ J84
                  ♣ KJ
                                 ♠ K7
                    N            ♡ J85
                  W   E          ◇ K975
                    S            ♣ 8652
```

West	North	East	South
−	−	−	1♣
Pass	1♡	Pass	1♠
Pass	3♠	Pass	4♠
All Pass			

Your partner leads the nine of spades against South's game. Dummy plays low and you win with your king. Plan the defence.

Gather the evidence: Partner has put you under a lot of pressure with his opening lead. You had to win the first trick and it now looks as if you have to find the killing switch with very little information to guide you.

Make a plan: If declarer has five solid club tricks he needs only a red-suit ace to bring his trick total up to ten (with three trumps and a red-suit ruff). If he is 2-2 in the red suits it does not matter what you do, but if he is 3-1 and his ace is singleton you could be in trouble if you lead the wrong suit. Partner's decision to lead a trump may not have been helpful but at least it looks as if he has tried to be helpful with his choice of card. The nine is surely his highest card in the suit and he is trying to suggest values in hearts.

Implement the plan: Play the jack of hearts. The full deal:

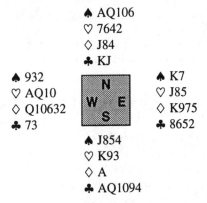

```
                 ♠ AQ106
                 ♡ 7642
                 ◇ J84
                 ♣ KJ
  ♠ 932                        ♠ K7
  ♡ AQ10         N             ♡ J85
  ◇ Q10632    W     E          ◇ K975
  ♣ 73           S             ♣ 8652
                 ♠ J854
                 ♡ K93
                 ◇ A
                 ♣ AQ1094
```

Note that because you needed three tricks in the suit it was necessary to switch to a high heart or declarer could simply have ducked your card.

2. Trump leads

One recurring problem against a suit contract is whether or not to lead trumps. Many players lead trumps because nothing else looks attractive – that is not generally advisable. Generally speaking we should always have a good reason for leading a trump and there is only any point in leading a trump if we can lead them often enough to be useful. The times when leading trumps is often a good idea is when the opponents are in a partscore and do not have a tremendous fit. In such a circumstance, the defenders will usually be on lead often enough to play trumps several times.

Sometimes the sequence suggests that a trump lead would be a good idea but our holding mitigates against such a choice. In the 1989 Bols Bridge Tips competition, Sandra Landy's tip was: Always have a good reason for leading trumps. If you have decided that a trump lead is right do not worry too much if your trump holding looks unsuitable.

North/South Game. Dealer West.

♠ K
♡ 107532
◊ K1053
♣ 853

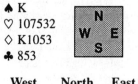

West	North	East	South
Pass	Pass	1◊	1♠
Double	2♠	2NT	4♠
Pass	Pass	Double	All Pass

Gather the evidence: Partner has shown a strong balanced hand with some spade values. South has done a lot of bidding vulnerable and is likely to have good distribution.

Make a plan: When your side has the balance of points and can be confident that the opposition do not have many long outside tricks, it is often right to lead a trump. On this deal it sounds as if the opponents have a 6-3 trump fit and it may well be a good idea to try to stop ruffs in dummy. It is not usually attractive to lead a singleton king but on this occasion partner has shown values in the suit so it may not matter. Even if it costs a trick, that trick may well come back later.

Implement the plan: Lead the king of spades. The full deal:

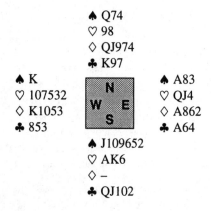

♠ Q74
♡ 98
◊ QJ974
♣ K97

♠ K
♡ 107532
◊ K1053
♣ 853

♠ A83
♡ QJ4
◊ A862
♣ A64

♠ J109652
♡ AK6
◊ –
♣ QJ102

If West leads a heart or a club, declarer makes his game easily. He ruffs a heart in the dummy and then plays trumps, later knocking out the ace of clubs to establish ten tricks.

After a diamond lead, dummy's diamonds are sufficient to prevent declarer being forced. The first trick goes to the queen, ace and declarer ruffs. He cashes the ace and king of hearts, ruffs a heart and plays a trump. West wins the king but cannot play diamonds to advantage.

On a spade lead the defenders must still be careful. West should read East's three as a suit-preference signal and switch to a club. (He also knows from the bidding that declarer is void in diamonds.) East can win and play ace and another spade and declarer has no chance.

Occasionally you are spoilt for choice, with a number of attractive holdings to choose from. However, if you follow Sandra's tip and the bidding calls for a trump lead, then that is what you should choose despite holding attractive sequential honour combinations in other suits.

East/West Game. Dealer South.

♠ QJ102
♡ AKJ
◇ 104
♣ 8652

West	North	East	South
–	–	–	1◇
Pass	1♡	Pass	1♠
Pass	2♣	Pass	2◇
Pass	2♠	Pass	3◇
Pass	4◇	Pass	4♡
Pass	4NT	Pass	5◇
Pass	6◇	All Pass	

Gather the evidence: It looks very much as if declarer is going to have a 4-1-6-2 distribution. Given your heart holding, his four heart bid must have been on a singleton. Dummy is probably 3-4-2-4 or 3-5-2-3.

Make a plan: If dummy is 3-4-2-4 there is a danger that you will be squeezed. If you lead a top heart you will have rectified the count for declarer and made his life easier. You could lead a spade but that is unlikely to achieve anything dramatic. The lead that is unlikely to give declarer anything and force him to make his own decisions about the hand is a trump.

Implement the plan: Lead the ten of diamonds. The full deal:

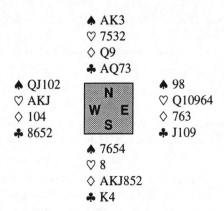

```
                    ♠ AK3
                    ♡ 7532
                    ◇ Q9
                    ♣ AQ73
        ♠ QJ102                      ♠ 98
        ♡ AKJ           N            ♡ Q10964
        ◇ 104       W       E        ◇ 763
        ♣ 8652          S            ♣ J109
                    ♠ 7654
                    ♡ 8
                    ◇ AKJ852
                    ♣ K4
```

A trump was led by Denmark's Soran Christiansen against Paul Chemla of France in the 1995 European Championship. Of course, Chemla could have given up a heart and played for a black-suit squeeze but he went for the simpler line of drawing trumps, discarding his heart on dummy's club, and then playing for spades 3-3. On the queen of spades lead declarer can play three rounds of clubs discarding a heart and then play ace and another spade, later ruffing a spade in the dummy.

3. Be sensible

When we are lucky enough to be on lead against a no trump contract with a good long suit there is still no guarantee that it is the right lead.

East/West Game. Dealer North.

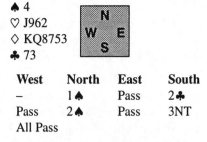

```
        ♠ 4
        ♡ J962          N
        ◇ KQ8753    W       E
        ♣ 73            S
```

West	North	East	South
–	1♠	Pass	2♣
Pass	2♠	Pass	3NT
All Pass			

Gather the evidence: The opponents' bidding sounds confident enough. Although you have no bad news for declarer in clubs, your spade holding suggests he may be disappointed in that suit.

Make a plan: It could be right to lead a diamond but the bidding suggests otherwise. Presumably South has a stopper in the suit and even if partner has a little help in diamonds you have no re-entry card. To be able to run the suit partner needs three diamonds and declarer two. It is much more likely that partner has some values in hearts. A spade lead is a possibility but is unlikely to do much good as you can't lead a second one.

Implement the plan: Lead the two of hearts. The full deal:

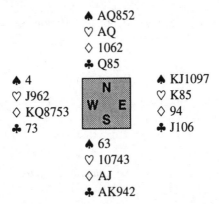

```
                    ♠ AQ852
                    ♡ AQ
                    ◇ 1062
                    ♣ Q85
        ♠ 4                      ♠ KJ1097
        ♡ J962        N          ♡ K85
        ◇ KQ8753   W     E       ◇ 94
        ♣ 73          S          ♣ J106
                    ♠ 63
                    ♡ 10743
                    ◇ AJ
                    ♣ AK942
```

The heart lead was found by Glyn Liggins in Britain's match against Belarus in the 1995 European Championship. As you can see, declarer had eight tricks on top and it was of paramount importance not to give him a trick on the lead as a diamond would have done.

Even if we do decide to lead our long suit it is often not clear whether to lead a low card or an honour.

Game All. Dealer South.

```
        ♠ 10954
        ♡ J7          N
        ◇ KQ1053   W     E
        ♣ 85          S
```

West	North	East	South
–	–	–	1♡
Pass	1♠	Pass	1NT
Pass	3NT	All Pass	

Gather the evidence: There is no way of knowing whether or not North/South have values to spare, but the bidding has sounded confident.

Make a plan: The percentages clearly favour a diamond lead but which one? A top honour could work well if one of the opponents holds jack doubleton. For a diamond lead to be positively successful (i.e. to beat the contract with diamond tricks rather than just give nothing away) you need to find partner either with the ace of diamonds or with at least three cards in the suit while declarer has ace doubleton. If partner has the ace of diamonds you would prefer to lead a low card in case his ace is doubleton; if declarer has ace doubleton, leading an honour will only succeed over a small card when he has ace-jack doubleton, surely against the odds.

Implement the plan: Lead the five of diamonds.

This deal occurred in the final of the 1989 Venice Cup. Karen McCallum for the USA led a low diamond while her counterpart for the Netherlands, chose the king. Dummy had Jxx and partner Ax, so the American lead was worth 12 IMPs.

Even against a suit contract, care sometimes needs to be taken in the selection of the right card.

Game All. Dealer East.

♠ 87
♡ K64
◇ 8532
♣ Q753

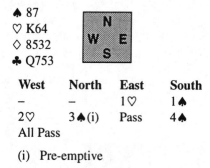

West	North	East	South
–	–	1♡	1♠
2♡	3♠(i)	Pass	4♠
All Pass			

(i) Pre-emptive

Gather the evidence: North's three spades was not really invitational, so South must have a very good overcall in order to bid on to game.

Make a plan: Partner has announced hearts as his longest suit and to lead anything else would be a wild guess. However, if you lead a low heart and one of the opponents has a singleton, as sounds likely on the bidding, you may never get the lead again. This may pose insuperable problems for your partner. If you lead your top heart you will probably retain the lead and may be able to find a useful switch.

Implement the plan: Lead the king of hearts. The full deal:

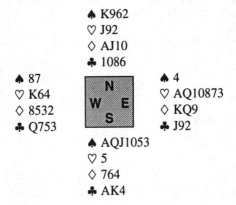

On the king of hearts your partner plays the queen, a clear suit-preference signal for a diamond. You switch to a diamond to partner's queen. Partner gets off play and there is nothing declarer can do. If he takes another diamond finesse, it will lose and he will still have to lose a club; if he exits with ace and another club you will win your queen and play another diamond.

Had you led a low heart partner would have won the ace and perhaps returned a heart. Declarer would have ruffed and drawn trumps ending in dummy, ruffed dummy's last heart and then played ace, king and another club. You would have won your queen and played a diamond but declarer would have ducked and your partner would have been endplayed.

4. Conventions

As we saw in the Introduction, our chosen method of honour-card leading against no trumps is one where the king and ten are strong.

We lead the king from such holdings that are so strong that we wish partner to unblock any honour card he holds and, failing that, to give count. Thus we would lead the king from KQJ10(x) obviously, but also from AKJ10.

	73			862			62	
AKJ10		Q52	AKJ10		9753	AKJ10		Q9753
	9864			Q4			84	

Partner will play the queen in the first instance, allowing us to cash four tricks, and the seven in the second case. If we can deduce partner has four cards rather than a doubleton we can continue the suit. In the third example, if partner plays the three and we know declarer cannot have four cards, after a negative response to Stayman for example, we can cash our five tricks.

We would also lead the king from KQ109x:

	xxx			Jxx	
KQ109x		Ax	KQ109x		Ax
	xxx			xxx	

In the first case partner will overtake and return the suit whereas in the second example he cannot afford to do so without establishing a trick for declarer, see the hand on page 45.

If the king asks for unblock or overtake then we have to choose a different card from a weaker holding. The card chosen is the queen but because we have a relatively weak holding we want partner to encourage or discourage. If we lead the queen from KQ9xx or KQ10x we would want partner to encourage with the jack or ace so that we could continue with a small one.

Our other leading convention against a no trump contract is that of the strong ten. This means that we lead the nine from 109xx but the ten from such holdings as KJ109x or A109xx. This method is often criticised because it gives away information to declarer. Such criticism is valid but, of course, it can also make life easy for us. Look how difficult this defensive problem would be playing normal leads:

Game All. Dealer South.

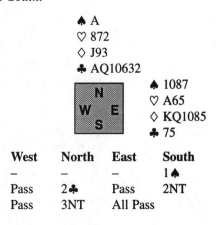

```
              ♠ A
              ♡ 872
              ◇ J93
              ♣ AQ10632
                              ♠ 1087
                              ♡ A65
                              ◇ KQ1085
                              ♣ 75
```

West	North	East	South
–	–	–	1♠
Pass	2♣	Pass	2NT
Pass	3NT	All Pass	

Partner leads the jack of hearts which you win with the ace, declarer playing the three. Plan the defence.

Gather the evidence: There really isn't very much. Declarer has at least 15 HCP with at least four spades. Partner might have led from a holding as weak J109x or as strong as KJ109x.

Make a plan: It could be right be to play a heart back. Perhaps the full deal is:

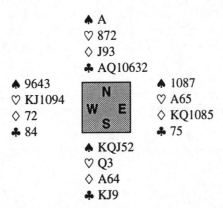

	♠ A	
	♡ 872	
	◇ J93	
	♣ AQ10632	
♠ 9643		♠ 1087
♡ KJ1094		♡ A65
◇ 72		◇ KQ1085
♣ 84		♣ 75
	♠ KQJ52	
	♡ Q3	
	◇ A64	
	♣ KJ9	

If you don't play a heart back straightaway declarer will make all the rest of the tricks.

Alternatively, perhaps the full deal is:

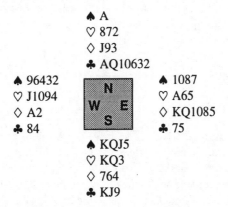

	♠ A	
	♡ 872	
	◇ J93	
	♣ AQ10632	
♠ 96432		♠ 1087
♡ J1094		♡ A65
◇ A2		◇ KQ1085
♣ 84		♣ 75
	♠ KQJ5	
	♡ KQ3	
	◇ 764	
	♣ KJ9	

Now it is essential to switch to a diamond. Once again, if you go wrong declarer will make all the rest of the tricks.

It is to help solve problems such as these that so many people like to play a method of opening leads such as strong tens. In the USA a system called 'zero or two higher' is very popular. This is just what it sounds like. From 109xx one would lead the ten, from KJ10x the ten, and from K109x the nine. This is probably an easier method for the defence, but also more of a giveaway to declarer than the strong ten method. I do not recommend it in this book except in a very specific circumstance that we will come to in the next chapter.

It is only recently that our trick-one signalling style against no trumps has been extended to suit contracts. It is becoming common in tournament bridge today: attitude on aces and queens, count on kings. This sounds straightforward enough. If partner leads an ace or a queen we tell him whether or not we like the suit; if he leads a king we tell him how many we have. The problem of course is for the opening leader. He has to decide whether or not he thinks he would like to know attitude or count.

The basic rule is that the more solid our holding and the higher the level of the final contract, the more likely we are to want to know count. Suppose we hold:

♠ 763
♡ AKQJ5
◊ 953
♣ 74

After the bidding sequence: 1NT – 4♠, we would choose the king of hearts. All we want to do is cash as many hearts as we can and then hope to find a penetrating switch. We can leave the rest to partner. On the other hand, suppose we hold:

♠ 763
♡ KQ76
◊ Q75
♣ Q95

The bidding has gone: 1NT – 2♠. If we are going to choose a heart it is likely that we want to know partner's attitude. If dummy comes down with Axx in hearts and our honour holds the first trick we want to know whether or not partner has the jack. The number of cards he holds in the suit is of much less importance. Also, as we have honours in both the other side-suits, it is more likely that we need to switch to one of those to set up some defensive tricks.

There is also the issue of leading the queen from king-queen at all since partner may confuse our holding with QJ10x. It is usually all right to be ambiguous against a partscore, but against a game contract we do not want to lead the queen from king-queen and watch partner overtake with his ace, fearing that declarer might have the singleton king. Later in the hand it may be obvious that you have the king-queen and so you can lead the queen more freely.

Against a slam, if we held an ace-king we would need to know whether both were cashing, hence we would lead the king for count, On the other hand, from Ax we wish to know whether partner has the king, hence ace for attitude.

It is not easy to know what information we want before we have seen dummy, but at least this method of signalling allows us the choice.

5. Bidding for the defence

One of the ways to improve the effectiveness of our partnership's opening leads is in the bidding. There are many ways to 'bid for the defence', the most basic of which is familiar to all of us – the simple overcall. We have all stuck our necks out to overcall on minimum values just to indicate an opening lead to partner. So far, we have mentioned gathering evidence from our bidding or lack of it, but have not considered that we can materially affect the choice of opening lead by taking some care in the bidding.

North/South Game. Dealer West.

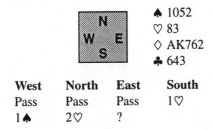

♠ 1052
♡ 83
♦ AK762
♣ 643

West	North	East	South
Pass	Pass	Pass	1♡
1♠	2♡	?	

This is another hand from Terence Reese's *Develop Your Bidding Judgment.* Your hand is worth a raise to two spades but there are two flaws in such a bid. Firstly, your hand is unsuitable for a sacrifice. You have two likely defensive tricks and none of your values in spades so you would have high hopes of defeating four hearts should the opponents bid it. The second flaw is that you do not wish to suggest a spade lead. The middle-of-the-road action would be to pass but there is much to be said for bidding three diamonds. Partner should realise that you cannot have a hand with a long diamond suit or you would have opened three diamonds in third seat at favourable vulnerability. He should appreciate that you have bid to influence his opening lead. In order for such a bid to have a measure of safety it must contain spade support. Should you find partner with a second suit in diamonds, then you would be happy for him to sacrifice after all.

Love All. Dealer South.

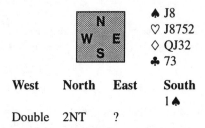 ♠ J8
♡ J8752
◇ QJ32
♣ 73

West	North	East	South
			1♠
Double	2NT	?	

Gather the evidence: North has shown a strong raise to at least three spades. It is unlikely, with your unexciting distribution, that your side would wish to sacrifice at Love All.

Make a plan: There can be only one purpose in bidding: to help your partner with his opening lead.

Implement the plan: Bid three diamonds. The full deal:

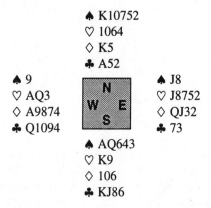

♠ K10752
♡ 1064
◇ K5
♣ A52

♠ 9   ♠ J8
♡ AQ3   ♡ J8752
◇ A9874   ◇ QJ32
♣ Q1094   ♣ 73

♠ AQ643
♡ K9
◇ 106
♣ KJ86

South bid four spades over three diamonds. West, Graham Kirby, started off with ace and another diamond and declarer had no chance, eventually

losing two hearts and a club as well as the ace of diamonds. John
Armstrong, East, did well to take advantage of North's two no trump bid.
At most tables North bid four spades to end the auction. Most Wests led a
club and declarer was now home.

You could argue that East/West were lucky. East's three diamond bid
would not have been written up as a triumph had the red kings been
swapped over. Knowing that his partner had diamond values there was a
very strong case for West to lead a trump, and it is surprising that he
didn't. From the bidding declarer will place East with any missing trump
honours.

It is the modern style to try to be as helpful as possible to partner when we
have a good fit. There are those who argue that such bidding can be more
helpful to the opponents than to partner; this is a matter of philosophy and
personality. I am sure that, in the long run, it is more important to help
partner. This can not only help him know whether to keep bidding but can
also help him with his opening lead. For example, suppose we hold the
following hand at Love All:

♠ 7
♡ Q652
◇ AQJ104
♣ 873

We pass as dealer and left-hand opponent opens one spade. Partner overcalls
two hearts and the next hand raises two spades. What should we bid?

Well, we are certainly worth four hearts. We have good four-card support
for partner's five-card (and very likely six) suit, a singleton in the
opponents' suit and a good source of tricks of our own. The problem is
that if we just bid four hearts it is very likely that the opponents will bid
four spades and partner will not know whether to bid on or pass (or
double). If he decides to defend he is likely to lead a heart which may not
be best for the defence. It is much more helpful to bid four diamonds. Now
if they bid four spades he can bid five hearts when he has:

♠ 852
♡ AK10873
◇ K53
♣ 10

Alternatively, he can double (or pass if he is conservative) and lead a
diamond when he holds:

♠ 852
♡ AK10873
◊ 3
♣ K105

These bids can be used after partner has opened the bidding as well as when he has overcalled. It is clearer that they must show a fit for partner when we are a passed hand but more and more pairs are choosing to play 'fit jumps' even when they have not already passed, using the argument that this is the most useful treatment of such a bid.

It is not only on such powerful hands that we can bid to help the defence. Consider the following bidding sequence:

West	North	East	South
–	–	–	1♡
1♠	2♡	?	

Suppose we hold either of the two hands below:

(a)	♠ 984	(b)	♠ K84
	♡ 762		♡ 762
	◊ K1073		◊ K1073
	♣ K84		♣ 984

On both hands we have the values for a simple raise, but there is no real need to bid for if partner has a very strong overcall he will bid again. With hand (a) we should pass and leave it up to partner; on hand (b) we want to help partner with his opening lead so bid two spades. Now if he is on lead against a heart contract he will feel happier about leading his broken suit.

Another useful way to bid for the defence is to double the opponents' conventional bids. Very often in the course of a bidding sequence the opponents will use fourth-suit forcing, a relay, a cue-bid, a response to Blackwood or some such. If we think that partner may end up on opening lead and we have a good holding in the conventional suit bid on our right, then we should double to suggest the lead to partner. If we don't double, partner is likely to choose between the other suits.

Sometimes we can even afford to double suits the opponents have bid naturally.

North/South Game. Dealer North.

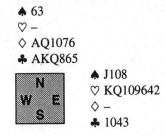

♠ J108
♡ KQ109642
◇ –
♣ 1043

West	North	East	South
	1♣	1♡	2♠
Pass	3◇	Pass	4NT
Pass	5♡	Pass	5NT
Pass	6◇	?	

You have taken a very conservative view of your hand so far. An immediate three heart overcall may have been more appropriate. However, here you have a chance to direct the defence. Double six diamonds. It is possible that six diamonds might make, but if North/South redouble you can always run to six hearts.

Over your double South bids six spades which ends the auction. Your partner leads the four of diamonds and dummy comes down:

♠ 63
♡ –
◇ AQ1076
♣ AKQ865

♠ J108
♡ KQ109642
◇ –
♣ 1043

Declarer rises with dummy's ace at trick one. You ruff. Plan the defence.

Gather the evidence: Declarer has used Blackwood so surely doesn't have a void. As he has made a grand slam try he must have the ace of hearts.

Make a plan: If declarer's trumps are solid he is threatening to draw trumps and run the club suit. He may not know that the suit is coming in, but we do. If his trumps are not solid the slam will go down anyway and we need not worry about that situation. The only possible defence is to hope that he has only a singleton club when a club switch now may thwart his plan.

Implement the plan: Switch to a club. The full deal:

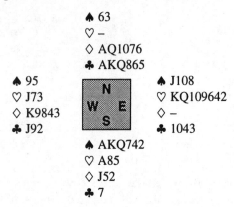

```
              ♠ 63
              ♡ –
              ◊ AQ1076
              ♣ AKQ865
♠ 95                              ♠ J108
♡ J73           N                 ♡ KQ109642
◊ K9843      W     E              ◊ –
♣ J92           S                 ♣ 1043
              ♠ AKQ742
              ♡ A85
              ◊ J52
              ♣ 7
```

Declarer cashes his three top clubs, discarding diamonds. He now leads a diamond from the dummy but you continue the good work by ruffing in with the ten of spades. Declarer can overruff, ruff a heart and play another diamond but you ruff in with the jack of spades and promote partner's nine.

You were lucky to find partner with the nine of spades but it was clear that, having ruffed the first diamond, no other defence would be successful.

One of the more tried and tested ways of trying to influence partner's opening lead, often against a slam, is to make a Lightner double, asking for an unusual lead. This usually suggests a void somewhere or else a strong holding in dummy's suit. In my experience, that is all very good in theory but in practice the Lightner double can be a very dangerous weapon, one that is only too likely to explode in the face of its user.

North/South Game. Dealer North.

```
                        ♠ A976
         N              ♡ –
      W     E           ◊ QJ10652
         S              ♣ 874
```

West	North	East	South
–	1♡	2◊	3♣
4◊	4NT	5◊	Double(i)
Pass	6♣	?	

(i)   One ace

Gather the evidence: The opponents have bid a slam despite some fairly heavy barrage from your side. However, they have used Blackwood so it is extremely unlikely that partner has an ace.

Make a plan: If partner can be persuaded to lead a heart there is every likelihood that the slam will go down as you would expect the ace of spades to stand up. Whether or not you decide to double must depend upon how likely you think it is that partner will lead a heart in any case. It is quite possible that a double may persuade the opponents to play in a contract that you cannot beat.

Implement the plan: OK, suppose you decide to double. The full deal:

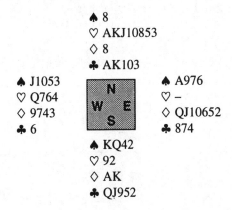

```
                ♠ 8
                ♡ AKJ10853
                ◊ 8
                ♣ AK103
  ♠ J1053                    ♠ A976
  ♡ Q764                     ♡ –
  ◊ 9743                     ◊ QJ10652
  ♣ 6                        ♣ 874
                ♠ KQ42
                ♡ 92
                ◊ AK
                ♣ QJ952
```

In the European Championships in Turku in 1989 East did indeed double six clubs. However, North was also aware of the likely outcome and bid six hearts. Aided by the knowledge that East was void in hearts for his Lightner double, declarer took a first-round heart finesse which was necessary to make the contract.

Here the risk was that the double would alert the opposition to the dangers of playing in six clubs and persuade them to remove to an unbeatable contract. That is not the only risk.

East/West Game. Dealer South.

```
                ♠ AKJ10942
                ♡ A3
                ◊ –
                ♣ KJ32
```

West	North	East	South
–	–	–	1♡
Pass	4♣(i)	4♠	Pass
Pass	5◇	Pass	5♡
Pass	Pass	?	

(i) Splinter

Gather the evidence: The opponents have stopped off in five hearts, having made a couple of slam tries en route. Your hand has so much defence that it looks likely that they have some extreme distribution.

Make a plan: You have one certain defensive trick in the ace of trumps and it does not sound as if either opponent is void in spades. Provided your partner can be persuaded to lead a diamond, five hearts should definitely go down.

Implement the plan: You double five hearts. The full deal:

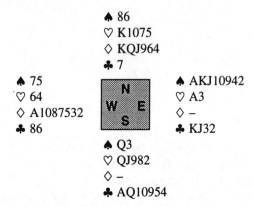

                    ♠ 86
                    ♡ K1075
                    ◇ KQJ964
                    ♣ 7

    ♠ 75   ♠ AKJ10942
    ♡ 64   ♡ A3
    ◇ A1087532   ◇ –
    ♣ 86   ♣ KJ32

                    ♠ Q3
                    ♡ QJ982
                    ◇ –
                    ♣ AQ10954

This deal comes from the 1989 Common Market Championships. West did as instructed and led the ace of diamonds which was not a success. Declarer ruffed and played the ace of clubs and ruffed a club. He now played a winning diamond, ruffed and overruffed. Another club ruff was followed by another winning diamond and East had to capitulate.

Note that had East not doubled West would have led a spade. Two rounds of spades followed by ace and another trump would have left declarer two down. Of course, West did not have to lead the *ace* of diamonds but that is another story ...

3
PARTNERSHIP CO-OPERATION

In the Introduction we laid out our basic method of signalling – primarily normal count (high-low shows an even number), but also attitude (high is encouraging) and suit preference. In this chapter we will build on these basic methods and add some more.

Partnership co-operation is really a question of confidence and that is built on agreements, as many as your memory allows, and knowing your partner – i.e. we need to know what he would do with a specific holding in a given situation. Does he tend to go for aggressive opening leads? Does he prefer to underlead queens or kings? Can we guess what he would lead from any hand after any sequence? Does he discard first from long suits or worthless ones? Can he be relied upon to play true cards all the time or does he sometimes forget or falsecard?

Much of this co-operation centres around signalling. We have already discussed count, attitude and suit preference. These are the three cornerstones on which all signalling is based, but the difficult part is deciding when which signal applies.

The main areas we are going to look at in this chapter are:

1. Suit preference
2. Some recent ideas in signalling
3. Making life easy for partner

1. Suit preference

(a) when partner has led a singleton

Game All. Dealer West.

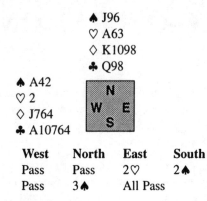

```
              ♠ J96
              ♡ A63
              ◊ K1098
              ♣ Q98
  ♠ A42
  ♡ 2          ┌─────────┐
  ◊ J764       │  N      │
  ♣ A10764     │ W     E │
               │    S    │
               └─────────┘
```

West	North	East	South
Pass	Pass	2♡	2♠
Pass	3♠	All Pass	

You lead your singleton heart to dummy's ace. Your partner plays the four and declarer the seven. Declarer now plays the six of spades to partner's three and his king. Plan the defence.

Gather the evidence: Partner has played his lowest heart at trick one. It is quite likely that he has only a singleton trump so nothing can be read into the three of spades.

Make a plan: Partner knew that your two of hearts was likely to be a singleton (no raise to three hearts) so has given you a suit-preference signal at trick one. He must have the king of clubs.

Implement the plan: Play a low club. The full deal:

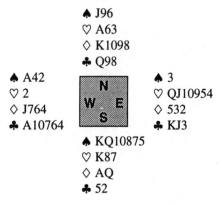

```
              ♠ J96
              ♡ A63
              ◊ K1098
              ♣ Q98
  ♠ A42        ┌─────────┐   ♠ 3
  ♡ 2          │  N      │   ♡ QJ10954
  ◊ J764       │ W     E │   ◊ 532
  ♣ A10764     │    S    │   ♣ KJ3
               └─────────┘
              ♠ KQ10875
              ♡ K87
              ◊ AQ
              ♣ 52
```

Partner will win his jack and play the five of hearts for you to ruff. You can then underlead your ace of clubs a second time for another ruff.

Obviously both players need to be aware of the singleton probability before the signal is suit preference or there can be confusion. The following situation caused a misunderstanding:

♡ J83

♡ 64   ♡ A1052

♡ KQ97

West led the six of hearts to his partner's ace and the two of hearts was returned. When East got in with his trump trick he returned the ten of hearts for his partner to ruff. However, West thought the two of hearts had been the suit-preference signal as his six might have been a singleton. In this situation there was no reason for East to suspect that the six of hearts was a singleton; in fact he thought it might have been from an honour, perhaps K96 or Q96. Accordingly he had returned his normal card, the fourth-highest two. It was only after the second round of the suit that he realised that his partner had led from shortage and only then that he showed suit preference.

(b) there is a singleton or source of tricks in dummy

A well-known suit-preference situation is when a top honour is led and dummy comes down with a singleton. This is because a switch is often important and there may be no other opportunity to suggest to partner which suit he should switch to. The same applies when the lead has set up such a source of tricks for declarer that a continuation is unthinkable. For example, suppose West leads an ace from ace doubleton and dummy shows up with KQJx in the suit; now all East's cards would be suit-preference signals.

Although the reason for giving a suit-preference signal when there is a singleton in dummy is because it is usually right for the defence to switch, this is not always the case and partner sometimes wants to be able to encourage the suit led. This can usually be done quite clearly.

Game All. Dealer West.

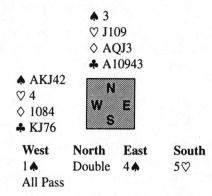

♠ 3
♡ J109
◇ AQJ3
♣ A10943

♠ AKJ42
♡ 4
◇ 1084
♣ KJ76

West	North	East	South
1♠	Double	4♠	5♡
All Pass			

You lead a top spade against five hearts. Partner plays the eight and declarer the seven. Plan the defence.

Gather the evidence: You cannot know the precise spade position but it is clear that the eight is not partner's highest card (he must have at least four cards in the suit so cannot have 865) and is unlikely to be his lowest (while he could have Q1098, he is much more likely to have a five-card suit at this vulnerability).

Make a plan: It would seem that partner does not have the king of diamonds or queen of clubs, in which case there is no purpose in playing either of those suits. The only place left for partner to hold any values is in trumps. If he holds good trumps, then you may be able to promote a trick for him by forcing dummy to ruff with one of its good intermediates.

Implement the plan: Play the king of spades. The full deal:

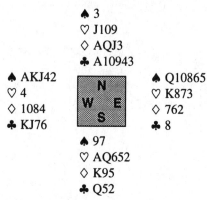

♠ 3
♡ J109
◇ AQJ3
♣ A10943

♠ AKJ42
♡ 4
◇ 1084
♣ KJ76

♠ Q10865
♡ K873
◇ 762
♣ 8

♠ 97
♡ AQ652
◇ K95
♣ Q52

Declarer must ruff the second spade with the nine of hearts but this promotes a trick for partner's eight. In the fullness of time the defence must also come to a club trick.

Note that had you switched to a diamond, say, declarer would have won in dummy, drawn trumps, played off his diamonds discarding a spade and would have just had to play clubs correctly to make his contract. He would certainly have deduced the club position because by the time he played the suit he would have had a good inferential count on both your hands.

(c) when we are giving a ruff

Love All. Dealer West.

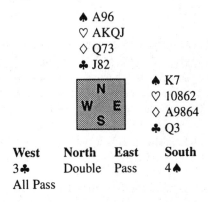

♠ A96
♥ AKQJ
♦ Q73
♣ J82

♠ K7
♥ 10862
♦ A9864
♣ Q3

West	North	East	South
3♣	Double	Pass	4♠
All Pass			

Partner leads the two of diamonds to your ace, declarer playing the king. Plan the defence.

Gather the evidence: It looks as if partner has a singleton diamond (J1052 is very unlikely) and it would certainly seem a good idea to start the defence by giving him a ruff.

Make a plan: Partner is going to be avidly watching the size of the card you return in order to locate your entry so he can get another ruff. You are more likely to get the lead with a club than a heart so perhaps you should return the four of diamonds. That would not be a good idea for the last thing you want partner to do is underlead his ace of clubs. You can see that you have a certain third defensive trick in the king of spades, so all you want partner to do is cash his ace of clubs. The way to do this is to signal enthusiastically for a heart, a suit that you can't possibly want. This clearly tells partner that you have nothing in clubs and therefore that it can't cost for him to cash the ace.

Implement the plan: Return the nine of diamonds. The full deal:

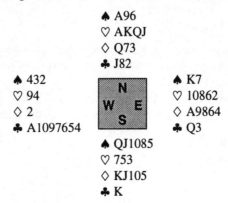

```
              ♠ A96
              ♡ AKQJ
              ◊ Q73
              ♣ J82
♠ 432                      ♠ K7
♡ 94          N            ♡ 10862
◊ 2        W     E         ◊ A9864
♣ A1097654    S            ♣ Q3
              ♠ QJ1085
              ♡ 753
              ◊ KJ105
              ♣ K
```

The only thing that could go wrong with your plan would be when partner had opened three clubs with a suit of K109xxx. However, in this instance, declarer would almost certainly have a doubleton heart to go with his doubleton club, in which case he would be able to discard a club loser on a winning heart. The only time it would be necessary for partner to switch to a club from the king would be when declarer had only four spades, say, ♠QJ10x ♡xxx ◊KJ10x ♣Ax. This is not a likely hand for him to have to jump to four spades; he surely would have preferred a four club cue-bid.

Sometimes we want to indicate to partner that our values are in neither of the outside suits, but rather that they are in trumps. This can be for a number of reasons.

Game All. Dealer South.

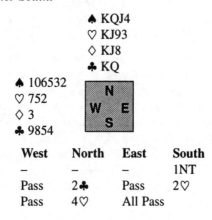

```
              ♠ KQJ4
              ♡ KJ93
              ◊ KJ8
              ♣ KQ
♠ 106532          N
♡ 752         W       E
◊ 3               S
♣ 9854
```

West	North	East	South
–	–	–	1NT
Pass	2♣	Pass	2♡
Pass	4♡	All Pass	

You lead your singleton diamond against South's four hearts. Your partner wins with the ace and returns the seven as declarer plays the four and the six. Plan the defence.

Gather the evidence: Probably declarer has at most four diamonds as he would be unlikely to open one no trump with a 2-4-5-2 shape. You know he has the queen. The seven cannot be partner's lowest diamond or his highest, therefore you do not expect him to hold a black-suit ace.

Make a plan: If partner doesn't hold a black-suit ace, the only way you can hope to beat four hearts is to find him with the ace of trumps. If you play a black suit there is a serious danger of declarer discarding dummy's remaining diamond on a club. It is important to play a trump now.

Implement the plan: Play the five of hearts. The full deal:

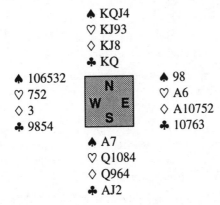

```
              ♠ KQJ4
              ♡ KJ93
              ◇ KJ8
              ♣ KQ
 ♠ 106532                      ♠ 98
 ♡ 752           N             ♡ A6
 ◇ 3          W     E          ◇ A10752
 ♣ 9854          S             ♣ 10763
              ♠ A7
              ♡ Q1084
              ◇ Q964
              ♣ AJ2
```

Had you idly got off play with, say, a club, declarer would have played three rounds of the suit discarding dummy's last diamond. Now he would have played a trump. Your partner would have won with the ace but when he played another diamond declarer would have been able to overruff in the dummy.

(d) giving suit preference with top honours

Game All. Dealer East.

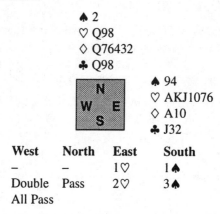

♠ 2
♡ Q98
◇ Q76432
♣ Q98

♠ 94
♡ AKJ1076
◇ A10
♣ J32

West	North	East	South
–	–	1♡	1♠
Double	Pass	2♡	3♠
All Pass			

Your partner leads the five of hearts against South's three spades and declarer plays low from dummy. Plan the defence.

Gather the evidence: Partner has led the highest outstanding heart and therefore has either a doubleton or a singleton. On the bidding he has shown a smattering of values.

Make a plan: It looks right to start with three rounds of hearts. However, you would like partner to know that your entry is in diamonds. In this type of situation you can signal with your honour cards, here playing the highest card you can afford at every opportunity.

Implement the plan: Win with the jack of hearts and then play the ace of hearts followed by the king. The full deal:

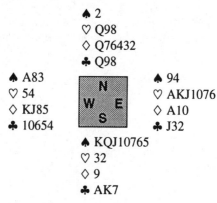

♠ 2
♡ Q98
◇ Q76432
♣ Q98

♠ A83
♡ 54
◇ KJ85
♣ 10654

♠ 94
♡ AKJ1076
◇ A10
♣ J32

♠ KQJ10765
♡ 32
◇ 9
♣ AK7

Declarer will probably ruff the third heart with the king of spades. Your partner should refuse to overruff. Now declarer will play another top trump. Your partner must win this with the ace and play a diamond to your ace. Now a fourth round of hearts will promote a trump trick.

Have you noticed that declarer has misplayed the hand? He should discard a diamond on the third heart. You would continue with a fourth round which he would ruff high. Now when he plays a trump your partner could win with the ace but would not be able to put you in for his trump promotion.

There is a valuable lesson here. Declarers are not perfect and some are less perfect than others. Even if a contract is unbeatable you will find that the better your defence, the more contracts will go down. Here you forced declarer to play correctly if he was to succeed. It is quite likely that several declarers misplayed at trick three but the Wests misdefended as well. Perhaps they overruffed the heart immediately, making the contract cold; or perhaps they passed that test and refused the overruff, but then, when they did win the ace of trumps, they guessed to put partner in with a club.

In the above situation it was easy for partner because he knew what our heart suit was. That is not always the case. Suppose we have bid hearts in the auction and eventually defend a spade contract. Suppose further that partner leads his singleton heart and the suit is distributed:

♡ 87

♡ 2   ♡ AJ10654

♡ KQ93

We win the ace and wish to return a suit-preference card for partner to ruff. We have shown a six-card suit in the bidding and cannot afford to play a low card for fear that declarer runs it round to the dummy and later has two valuable discards. Suppose we wish partner to return the higher-ranking suit and play the jack. How can partner know that the suit is not:

♡ 87

♡ 2   ♡ AQJ654

♡ K1093

In addition, suppose we wish partner to return the lower-ranking suit, and play the ten. Again, how can partner know that the suit is not:

♡ 87
♡ 2   ♡ A109654
♡ KQJ3

One solution is that the queen and ten should be arbitrarily ascribed high-card status and the jack and nine ascribed low-card status. Thus a suit-preference signal for the higher suit would be the ten, queen and ten on the above three examples, where suit preference for the lower suit would be the jack, jack and nine.

This situation will not arise often but this may be a very useful agreement when it does.

(e) secondary suit-preference signals

We have looked at a number of different situations where suit-preference signals work well but possibly the most useful is in the general, routine play of our inconsequential spot cards. If you have, say, 743 in a suit you start by playing the three to tell partner that you have an odd number but on the next occasion have a free choice between the seven and the four. Help partner with a suit-preference signal. If you have 7543 you would start with the second highest, the five, to show four and on the next round would be able to choose between the four and the three (the seven would not be a good idea as partner might not be able to tell that you had begun a peter).

Game All. Dealer North.

♠ AKQJ5
♡ 72
◇ J83
♣ J64

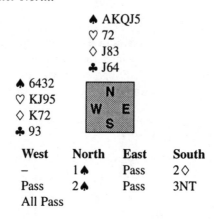

♠ 6432
♡ KJ95
◇ K72
♣ 93

West	North	East	South
–	1♠	Pass	2◇
Pass	2♠	Pass	3NT
All Pass			

You lead the five of hearts to your partner's ace and declarer's six. He returns the three of hearts to the ten and your jack. You cash the king and nine of hearts, partner playing the four and eight, whilst dummy discarded a club and a diamond and declarer a club. Plan the defence.

Gather the evidence: Partner's original heart holding was A842. He returned the two to show he had four but thereafter had a free choice between the four and the eight. It is quite possible that he holds no other high card as declarer could easily have a 17-count for his bidding. However, if he does have another honour it must be in clubs for with a preference for diamonds he would have played the eight before the four (clearly spades are out of the picture on this occasion).

Make a plan: The only hand for declarer that would have necessitated you being active at this stage of the defence was, for example, ♠10 ♡Q106 ◇Q10xxx ♣AKQx. Had this been declarer's hand you would have needed to cash two diamonds quickly. However, partner has told you that declarer does not hold this hand so you can afford to be passive.

Implement the plan: Play the six of spades. The full deal:

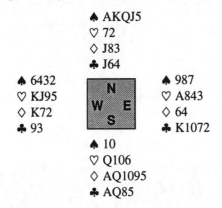

```
                  ♠ AKQJ5
                  ♡ 72
                  ◇ J83
                  ♣ J64
  ♠ 6432                        ♠ 987
  ♡ KJ95          N             ♡ A843
  ◇ K72        W     E          ◇ 64
  ♣ 93            S             ♣ K1072
                  ♠ 10
                  ♡ Q106
                  ◇ AQ1095
                  ♣ AQ85
```

Note that just because partner told you that he (probably) had values in clubs did not mean that he wanted you to play the suit. On the contrary, that would have been a way to hand declarer three club tricks. As soon as you knew partner did not have the ace of diamonds you could afford to sit back and wait.

This co-operation can often be very subtle.

Love All. Dealer East.

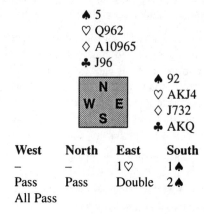

♠ 5
♡ Q962
◇ A10965
♣ J96

♠ 92
♡ AKJ4
◇ J732
♣ AKQ

West	North	East	South
–	–	1♡	1♠
Pass	Pass	Double	2♠
All Pass			

Partner leads the five of hearts against South's two spades. You win with the jack, declarer playing the three. You cash the king of hearts (showing your club preference) and partner plays the ten. Plan the defence.

Gather the evidence: Even though you have shown preference for clubs, partner has suggested that you play diamonds. Looking at that dummy it seems unlikely that it should be a necessary thing to do.

Make a plan: You can see five probable defensive tricks – two hearts and three clubs. If partner has a trump trick it will appear in the fullness of time. There are two other possibilities for an extra trick. Perhaps partner has king doubleton of diamonds, in which case, if you defend passively, he will come to his diamond trick at the end.

The other possibility is not so easy to see. If declarer has a singleton diamond and four clubs you may be able to prevent him coming to a long club trick. Partner would not have signalled so strongly with just one diamond honour when there was such a powerful holding in dummy, so it must be best to switch to a diamond.

Implement the plan: Play the two of diamonds. The full deal:

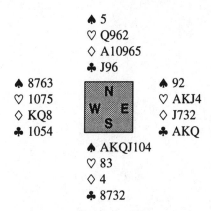

```
                  ♠ 5
                  ♡ Q962
                  ◇ A10965
                  ♣ J96
  ♠ 8763                        ♠ 92
  ♡ 1075          N             ♡ AKJ4
  ◇ KQ8         W   E           ◇ J732
  ♣ 1054          S             ♣ AKQ
                  ♠ AKQJ104
                  ♡ 83
                  ◇ 4
                  ♣ 8732
```

Declarer will win partner's queen with the ace and perhaps draw trumps. Now he will play a club. You will win with the queen and play another diamond. He will ruff and play a second club. You will win with the king and play another diamond. He will ruff with his last trump and play another club. You will win with the ace and cash the ace of hearts. There are variations if he plays clubs before trumps but declarer cannot succeed. Had you played just one high club you would have let declarer make his contract.

2. Some new ideas in signalling

(a) the 'obvious switch'

This is a new signalling method, well described in a recent publication, *A Switch in Time*, by Matthew and Pamela Granovetter. I will not go into it in any detail here and if you are interested in adopting it you should buy the book. However, the theory rests on the premise that when you lead an honour that may hold the trick, dummy usually contains a suit that could be called an 'obvious switch'. Now the attitude signal of the player over dummy refers to the 'obvious switch' suit not the suit led.

We will start by looking at the following problem using normal suit preference.

Game All. Dealer West.

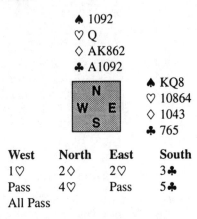

♠ 1092
♡ Q
◇ AK862
♣ A1092

♠ KQ8
♡ 10864
◇ 1043
♣ 765

West	North	East	South
1♡	2◇	2♡	3♣
Pass	4♡	Pass	5♣
All Pass			

West leads the king of hearts against South's five clubs. Plan the defence.

Gather the evidence: Looking at the dummy it would seem that the best chance for further defensive tricks is in spades.

Make a plan: It may not be so obvious to partner. If he holds the ace of spades, he may be worried about giving declarer a trick with the king of that suit. It is important to tell partner that you have a strong spade holding. Your signalling method, as outlined at the beginning of this book and in this chapter, is suit preference when there is a singleton in dummy.

Implement the plan: Play the ten of hearts. The full deal:

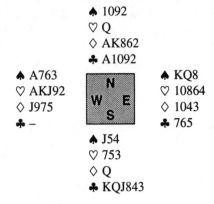

♠ 1092
♡ Q
◇ AK862
♣ A1092

♠ A763
♡ AKJ92
◇ J975
♣ –

♠ KQ8
♡ 10864
◇ 1043
♣ 765

♠ J54
♡ 753
◇ Q
♣ KQJ843

This time there is no problem. Partner switches to a spade and five clubs goes two down.

Note that had your hand been ♠QJ8 ♡10864 ◇Q104 ♣752, a spade switch would have let declarer make his contract whereas a heart continuation (or diamond shift) would have left him with no chance.

Those advocates of the 'obvious switch' method would play a high heart here to encourage the 'obvious switch', spades. With a less robust spade holding they would play a low heart to discourage *spades* and leave the rest up to partner. The drawback with this method is that partner may not be able to tell between switching to the 'non-obvious' suit, a trump or a continuation of the first suit. As against that, it is easier to give a clear message. Often declarer can play a false card and make it difficult to tell whether partner has given suit preference or played a middle card.

A further point to be taken into account when considering taking up a new signalling method is one of tempo. If it takes a long time to decide what card to play at trick one, partner is going to be put in a difficult ethical position. We need to feel confident that this is a temporary problem that we will soon overcome.

(b) Smith peters

The Smith peter is an extremely useful tool, used by many expert pairs. The idea is that after the opening lead against a no trump contract, a peter by either defender in the first suit played by declarer suggests that he would like partner to continue with this suit when he is next on lead (though there are variations). The corollary of this is that a failure to peter suggests that a switch would be a good idea.

The peter must be used in the context of the whole hand and what is already known about the respective holdings in the suit.

Game All. Dealer South.

♠ 10972
♡ 8
◇ Q76
♣ KJ987

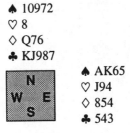

♠ AK65
♡ J94
◇ 854
♣ 543

West	North	East	South
–	–	–	1♡
Pass	1♠	Pass	3NT
All Pass			

West leads the three of diamonds against South's three no trumps. South wins with the jack in hand and plays the queen of spades, West contributing the three. Plan the defence.

Gather the evidence: Partner's three of spades must be his lowest card from two or three small.

Make a plan: Partner is trying to tell you that he does not want you to continue with diamonds. Looking at the dummy this is bound to be because he has a good heart holding. It will be most useful for him if you switch to a high heart.

Implement the plan: Play the jack of hearts. The full deal:

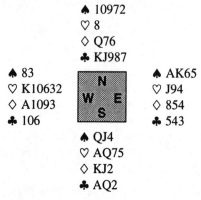

```
                    ♠ 10972
                    ♡ 8
                    ◊ Q76
                    ♣ KJ987
    ♠ 83                            ♠ AK65
    ♡ K10632        N               ♡ J94
    ◊ A1093      W     E            ◊ 854
    ♣ 106           S               ♣ 543
                    ♠ QJ4
                    ♡ AQ75
                    ◊ KJ2
                    ♣ AQ2
```

Declarer has no chance of making his contract and will surely go two down.

Had partner's hand been ♠83 ♡Q1063 ◊A10932 ♣106 he would have played the eight of spades first and you would have known to press on with diamonds.

As with any other form of signal, it is important to consider the whole hand, not just one particular suit.

Game All. Dealer South.

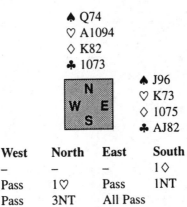

♠ Q74
♡ A1094
◇ K82
♣ 1073

♠ J96
♡ K73
◇ 1075
♣ AJ82

West	North	East	South
–	–	–	1◇
Pass	1♡	Pass	1NT
Pass	3NT	All Pass	

Partner leads the two of spades against South's three no trumps. Declarer wins with the queen in dummy and plays a low diamond to his queen, partner playing the three. Declarer now runs the queen of hearts to your king, partner playing the six. Which diamond did you play at trick two? Plan the rest of the defence.

Gather the evidence: On another day it may have been a good idea to peter in diamonds to tell partner about the jack of spades, the best possible card given the play to trick one. However, the possibility of an advantageous club switch is quite high so the five of diamonds was a better choice.

Partner has shown four spades, four hearts and has also suggested that there may be a better defence than a spade continuation (the three of diamonds).

Make a plan: There is a high probability that declarer will have nine tricks when he has dislodged your king of hearts. You know of two spades and three hearts and it looks likely that he has at least four diamond tricks. You cannot afford to duck the heart in case he has a five-card diamond suit when he will only need two heart tricks. It is imperative to try to take some club tricks. It is likely that partner has the king of clubs but you may need to be careful to take four tricks in the suit. If partner has a doubleton club you cannot manage this so you have to hope he has three. You also need him to have the nine.

Implement the plan: Win the king of hearts and play the jack of clubs. The full deal:

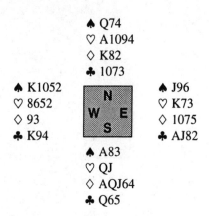

♠ Q74
♡ A1094
◊ K82
♣ 1073

♠ K1052
♡ 8652
◊ 93
♣ K94

♠ J96
♡ K73
◊ 1075
♣ AJ82

♠ A83
♡ QJ
◊ AQJ64
♣ Q65

Declarer will no doubt cover with the queen and when partner returns the nine of clubs declarer has no chance. He must lose four club tricks and the king of hearts.

(c) leads after trick one

Many players revert to normal leads after trick one, but 'ace for attitude, king for count' is even more useful. Leads are still low from honours and second from small cards, but sometimes count in the suit partner is leading is more critical than whether or not he has an honour.

North/South Game. Dealer North.

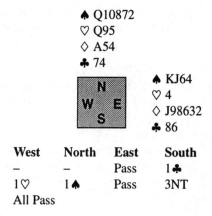

♠ Q10872
♡ Q95
◊ A54
♣ 74

♠ KJ64
♡ 4
◊ J98632
♣ 86

West	North	East	South
–	–	Pass	1♣
1♡	1♠	Pass	3NT
All Pass			

Much to your surprise, your partner does not lead his own suit, rather he leads yours. He starts with the queen, followed by the king, of diamonds, declarer ducking twice in dummy. You play the nine of diamonds on the second round to show your spade values – after all, it is likely that both declarer and partner have doubleton diamonds as declarer would probably not have bid three no trumps with a small singleton. Partner switches to the three of spades and dummy plays the seven. Plan the defence.

Gather the evidence: Declarer's three no trump bid is surely based on a long good club suit. Your partner is on your side and is trying to tell you something when he switches to a low card.

Make a plan: When partner switches to a low card it is usually because he has an honour in the suit. However, in this case that is most unlikely. If partner has the ace of spades declarer must have most of the rest of the high cards. He would not risk losing the first five tricks in a contract where he had nine top tricks or where he would have nine tricks if a club finesse were right. Declarer must have the ace of spades because partner would have played it if he had it. If partner does not have the ace of spades he must be trying to tell us that he has three cards in the suit rather than a doubleton.

Implement the plan: Play the six of spades. The full deal:

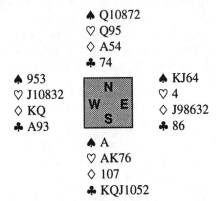

                    ♠ Q10872
                    ♡ Q95
                    ◊ A54
                    ♣ 74
    ♠ 953   ♠ KJ64
    ♡ J10832   ♡ 4
    ◊ KQ   ◊ J98632
    ♣ A93   ♣ 86
                    ♠ A
                    ♡ AK76
                    ◊ 107
                    ♣ KQJ1052

Declarer wins with the ace and plays the king of clubs but partner wins with the ace and plays another spade so you take five winners.

You have combined well as a partnership: partner found a good opening lead; you did well to give him a suit-preference signal; he was helpful to give you a count in spades which enabled you to find the winning defence of ducking on the first round.

The following situation has posed problems for most partnerships at some time or other.

Game All. Dealer South.

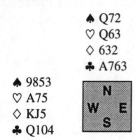

♠ Q72
♡ Q63
◊ 632
♣ A763

♠ 9853
♡ A75
◊ KJ5
♣ Q104

South's opening one no trump is passed out. You lead the eight of spades which partner wins with the ace. He then switches to the jack of hearts and declarer plays low. Plan the defence.

Gather the evidence: Partner has either led from J109x or KJ10x. If the former you must play small or you give declarer two heart tricks; if the latter you must play the ace or you give declarer a heart trick to which he is not entitled.

Make a plan: Consider the defence from partner's viewpoint. To switch to a heart from KJ10x(x) with Q63 in the dummy is a very panicky play. It cannot be necessary to take four (or five) heart tricks at this particular moment – and if it were necessary partner should duck the ace of spades to give you a chance to signal. It is much more likely that partner's hearts are headed by the jack.

Implement the plan: Play the five of hearts. The full deal:

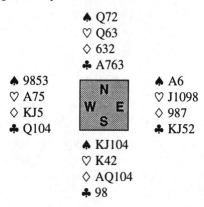

♠ Q72
♡ Q63
◊ 632
♣ A763

♠ 9853
♡ A75
◊ KJ5
♣ Q104

♠ A6
♡ J1098
◊ 987
♣ KJ52

♠ KJ104
♡ K42
◊ AQ104
♣ 98

Some pairs like to retain a 'strong ten' leading style to overcome this problem. Though remember that if partner had KJ10x over Qxx in dummy and he really needed to play you for the ace to have any hope of defeating a contract he should switch to his fourth highest, giving you no real option but to win your ace.

Another situation that recurs against a no trump contract is when dummy is unexpectedly extremely short (singleton or void) in a suit. Thus the obvious defence is to attack this suit whatever our holding. For example, suppose the bidding has been:

West	North	East	South
			1NT
Pass	2♣	Pass	2♠
Pass	3NT	All Pass	

Partner leads the six of hearts and dummy comes down with:

♠ –
♡ KQ95
◊ KQ632
♣ K843

Our hand is one of the following:

(a) ♠ KJ109   (b) ♠ J1098   (c) ♠ J1032
    ♡ AJ874   ♡ AJ874   ♡ AJ1087
    ◊ 54   ◊ 54   ◊ 54
    ♣ J5   ♣ A5   ♣ A5

In each instance we decide to win to lead a high spade in order to force declarer to cover, but if we lead the jack from each hand and declarer plays the queen, how is partner supposed to know what to do when he holds:

♠ A7654
♡ 63
◊ 1087
♣ 97

If we have either (a) or (b), it is essential for him to play a spade back; if we have (c) then he must go back to hearts. You may say that we should switch to a low spade when we have a weaker holding such as in (c), but suppose partner's hand was:

♠ AQ984
♡ 63
◇ J62
♣ 972

Now it would be essential to lead an honour. If we play a low spade, declarer will simply duck to partner's hand.

This is a very difficult situation to get right all the time but we can give ourselves a better chance. There is a method of opening leads that is currently in vogue in the USA whereby the lead of the nine, ten, jack or queen shows 'zero or two higher'. This means exactly what it says: from QJx the queen; from KJ10 lead the ten; from K109 lead the nine. One of the problems with this method is that it can help declarer more than it does partner. However, it can usefully be applied to this situation. Using such a method, you would play the ten of spades on (a), the nine on (b) and the jack on (c). Partner would know that on (a) you had either KJ10x or 109xx, on (b) K109x, Q109x, J109x or 98xx and on (c) J10xx at best. Although he will still not get it right all the time, he is in a much better position to judge.

(d) wake partner up

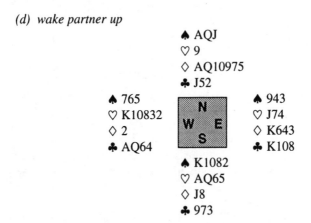

```
                    ♠ AQJ
                    ♡ 9
                    ◇ AQ10975
                    ♣ J52
    ♠ 765              N         ♠ 943
    ♡ K10832                     ♡ J74
    ◇ 2         W         E      ◇ K643
    ♣ AQ64           S           ♣ K108
                    ♠ K1082
                    ♡ AQ65
                    ◇ J8
                    ♣ 973
```

Both tables reached three no trumps by South in this deal from the 1995 Camrose match between England and Wales. A heart was led at both tables. In the Closed Room, where the contract was doubled, the English East switched to the eight of clubs when he won the king of diamonds. His partner won the queen but, thinking his partner did not have an honour in clubs and therefore did have the king of spades, switched back to hearts. Declarer made eleven tricks for +750 to Wales.

In the Open Room the early play was the same but on the second diamond West, Tony Ratcliff, discarded the king of hearts! Declarer was now marked with the ace of hearts so a heart continuation would concede the game. The only chance was to take four club tricks so East switched to the king of clubs, leaving no room for partner to go wrong. Wales gained 50 and 13 IMPs.

We must not forget, however, that we can have all the conventions in the world but what is really most important of all is to reduce partner's chance of error when we know what to do.

3. Making it easy for partner

It is not enough to work out how to defend a hand; we must communicate that knowledge to partner. Sometimes we can use a convention such as leading a king when we have a singleton, an example of which was given in the chapter on strategy. We boost partnership confidence by making life easier for partner, possibly forcing him to do the right thing.

North/South Game. Dealer North.

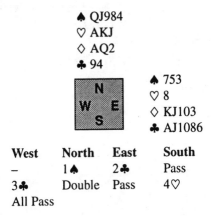

```
              ♠ QJ984
              ♡ AKJ
              ◇ AQ2
              ♣ 94
                              ♠ 753
          N                   ♡ 8
        W   E                 ◇ KJ103
          S                   ♣ AJ1086
```

West	North	East	South
–	1♠	2♣	Pass
3♣	Double	Pass	4♡
All Pass			

Your partner leads the five of clubs against South's four hearts. You win with the ace and declarer plays the two. Plan the defence.

Gather the evidence: It looks as if partner has either ♣K75 or ♣Q75. It is a pity you stretched to make such an aggressive overcall as you would have preferred a diamond lead.

Make a plan: You must hope that partner has the king of clubs. Declarer will surely be able to establish some spade tricks for diamond discards so it is important that partner gets the lead now. The natural card to return is the jack of clubs but a bright declarer might duck that and leave you on lead.

Implement the plan: Return the eight of clubs. The full deal:

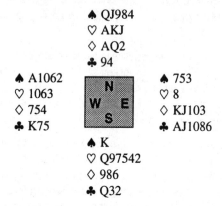

♠ QJ984
♡ AKJ
◇ AQ2
♣ 94

♠ A1062   ♠ 753
♡ 1063   ♡ 8
◇ 754   ◇ KJ103
♣ K75   ♣ AJ1086

♠ K
♡ Q97542
◇ 986
♣ Q32

When partner is forced to win the king of clubs he will surely work out to switch to a diamond. It was unlikely that a discard from dummy on the queen of clubs would matter given dummy's spade suit. It is true that, had you played the jack of clubs and declarer had declined to cover, partner could have saved you by overtaking with his king. But why put him to the test? A good defender always tries to make life easy for his partner.

Game All. Dealer East.

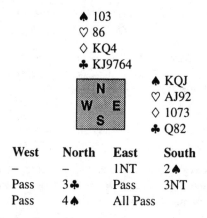

♠ 103
♡ 86
◇ KQ4
♣ KJ9764

♠ KQJ
♡ AJ92
◇ 1073
♣ Q82

West	North	East	South
–	–	1NT	2♠
Pass	3♣	Pass	3NT
Pass	4♠	All Pass	

Your partner leads the five of hearts against South's game. You win with the ace and declarer plays the ten. Plan the defence.

Gather the evidence: You can see three defensive tricks and the fourth must come from one of the minors – partner must have an ace.

Make a plan: It looks natural to return a heart or a spade but try to look at the hand from partner's point of view. If he has the ace of diamonds it cannot disappear quickly, but suppose he has the ace of clubs. He does not know that you have two trump tricks to go with your ace of hearts. Even if you lead a spade this will not be clear. You want to make sure that he does not duck his ace of clubs when the time comes. From his perspective this may be the best chance for declarer to go wrong.

Implement the plan: Play the two of clubs. The full deal:

♠ 103
♡ 86
◊ KQ4
♣ KJ9764

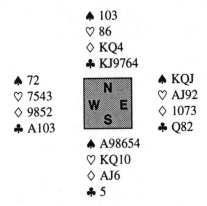

♠ 72   ♠ KQJ
♡ 7543   ♡ AJ92
◊ 9852   ◊ 1073
♣ A103   ♣ Q82

♠ A98654
♡ KQ10
◊ AJ6
♣ 5

When you switch to the two of clubs, partner will know that declarer has a singleton.

Conversely if you don't know what to do, then let partner make the decision.

Love All. Dealer North.

♠ AJ42
♡ AQ
◊ 643
♣ AQ103

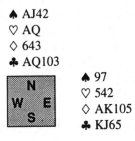

♠ 97
♡ 542
◊ AK105
♣ KJ65

West	North	East	South
–	1♣	Pass	1♠
Pass	3♠	All Pass	

Your partner leads the queen of diamonds on which you play a discouraging five. He obediently switches to the seven of clubs to the queen and king, declarer playing the two. Plan the defence.

Gather the evidence: It is not clear whether partner has a singleton club. He may think that he was on lead for the last time and want to be helpful rather than just blindly continue with diamonds.

Make a plan: You need to try to find a way to find out whether he has a singleton club. If there was a way to give him the option of being on lead or not you could be confident that if he chose to be on lead he would not have a singleton, whereas if he left you on lead than he would be suggesting that he wanted a ruff. The one card that you do know he has is the jack of diamonds.

Implement the plan: Play the ten of diamonds. The full deal:

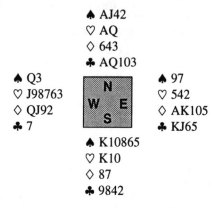

```
                    ♠ AJ42
                    ♡ AQ
                    ◇ 643
                    ♣ AQ103
      ♠ Q3             N          ♠ 97
      ♡ J98763     W       E      ♡ 542
      ◇ QJ92           S          ◇ AK105
      ♣ 7                          ♣ KJ65
                    ♠ K10865
                    ♡ K10
                    ◇ 87
                    ♣ 9842
```

To defeat three spades you need two tricks in each minor and either a club ruff or a trump trick. If the ten of diamonds holds the trick you should play a club, expecting to give partner a ruff. On the other hand, if partner does not have a singleton club he should overtake the diamond and take charge of the defence himself. Of course, declarer was greedy but no-one is perfect and you have to take advantage of opponents' errors.

To round off this chapter we will look at a hand that cropped up in the World Junior Championship in 1995.

Love All. Dealer South.

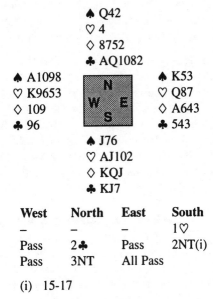

♠ Q42
♡ 4
◊ 8752
♣ AQ1082

♠ A1098   ♠ K53
♡ K9653   ♡ Q87
◊ 109   ◊ A643
♣ 96   ♣ 543

♠ J76
♡ AJ102
◊ KQJ
♣ KJ7

West	North	East	South
–	–	–	1♡
Pass	2♣	Pass	2NT(i)
Pass	3NT	All Pass	

(i) 15-17

West led the ten of spades against three no trumps. What is required is for East to play the king of spades and switch to a heart. Declarer must duck this or he sets up two heart tricks for the defence to go with two spades and the ace of diamonds. West wins the king of hearts and continues with a low spade. Now the defence can take two more spade tricks when East gets in with the ace of diamonds. Very difficult, but the defenders might reason along these lines:

East: 'Partner probably does not have a good five-card spade suit as he has some values and did not bid over South's one heart. His spades are likely to be 109xx(x) or A109x. If partner's spades are just 109xx(x), then declarer has two spade tricks, probably five clubs and it would be surprising if he did not have two tricks in the red suits. If partner's spades are A109x there are more possibilities. I can already see four defensive tricks but where is the fifth? I must play partner for a red-suit king.

If partner has the king of diamonds, it is quite likely that declarer can take nine tricks straight away (one spade, three hearts with the aid of a finesse and five clubs), so I must play partner for the king of hearts. However, if I play the king of spades and return a spade, partner may duck to keep communications open and declarer will play a diamond; when I take my ace declarer will also have nine tricks (one spade, one heart, two diamonds and five clubs). If partner has the king of hearts I can defend better by winning the king of spades and playing a heart. I had better switch to the eight of hearts as I don't want partner to continue the suit.'

West: 'Partner has played the king of spades at trick one, which is an unusual card to play when I have led the ten and the queen is in dummy. However, it was clearly important for him to be on lead. He has switched to a high heart so he doesn't want me to continue with that suit. If he had a good diamond suit, surely he would have switched to that instead. If he started with three spades I can see a straightforward way to beat the contract provided he has one entry. I can continue with a low spade. When he gets in with his minor-suit entry he can play another spade and I will take two tricks in the suit.'

There are many hands where the successful defence is of this type but they are very difficult to get right at the table. If partner makes an opening lead in a suit in which we have some length and a top honour, it seems right to continue that suit. If we make a lead and partner does find the winning switch it is not always easy to see that we have to revert to the original suit.

4
EXPERT TECHNIQUE

In *Step-by-Step: Planning the Defence* we looked at some areas of basic technique:

- *counting* – tricks, points, distribution
- *communications* – keeping our own open and cutting declarer's
- *trump play* – taking ruffs, drawing trumps, forcing declarer to ruff, trump control, withholding trumps, trump promotions

In this book we are going to expand some of these themes. The subjects we shall look at are:

1. Ducking
2. Coups
3. Specific card chosen
4. Attacking communications
5. Avoiding the squeeze/endplay

1. Ducking

There are many reasons for ducking. A classic example is when the suit lay-out is:

```
                    KQxxx
        xx                     AJx
                    xxx
```

Declarer leads low to dummy's queen. If we win as East, declarer will duck on the next round and be able to make three tricks in the suit even if dummy has no entries. If we let declarer make the first trick in the suit that will be the only one he does make (if dummy is entryless).

We would all believe this to be straightforward and yet at the table we do not live up to our own expectations. Here are two Internationals mishandling this combination:

East/West Game. Dealer North.

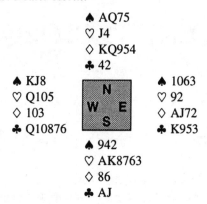

```
                    ♠ AQ75
                    ♡ J4
                    ◊ KQ954
                    ♣ 42
    ♠ KJ8                        ♠ 1063
    ♡ Q105          N            ♡ 92
    ◊ 103        W     E         ◊ AJ72
    ♣ Q10876        S            ♣ K953
                    ♠ 942
                    ♡ AK8763
                    ◊ 86
                    ♣ AJ
```

At both tables in a 1996 Camrose match a club was led against four hearts. Both declarers ducked East's king and both defenders switched to a trump. The Souths won and played a diamond. It looks clear, on general principles, for East to duck this but both players won, despite having been given accurate count by partner. The Scottish East switched to a spade so the game went down anyway, but the English East continued with a trump and declarer eventually set up a long diamond to dispose of his spade loser.

The most common reason for ducking is simply to make declarer guess the location of the high cards. If we duck smoothly declarer will tend not to place us with the missing high card. If we win declarer will know for certain what honour we have been dealt. This can help him, not only in that suit, but also to make general inferences about the hand.

Love All. Dealer South.

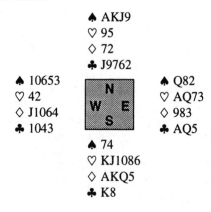

```
                    ♠ AKJ9
                    ♡ 95
                    ◊ 72
                    ♣ J9762
    ♠ 10653                      ♠ Q82
    ♡ 42            N            ♡ AQ73
    ◊ J1064      W     E         ◊ 983
    ♣ 1043          S            ♣ AQ5
                    ♠ 74
                    ♡ KJ1086
                    ◊ AKQ5
                    ♣ K8
```

West	North	East	South
–	–	–	1♡
Pass	1♠	Pass	1NT
Pass	2NT	Pass	3NT
All Pass			

West led the jack of diamonds and declarer won the ace to lead a low spade to dummy's nine. East ducked. Declarer now played the nine of hearts, ducked all around and a second heart went to declarer's ten. Next he played the king of clubs which East won to return a diamond. Declarer won and played his low club to dummy's jack. East won with the queen and returned his last diamond. When declarer won and took the 'sure' spade finesse, East won the queen and cashed the ace of hearts before playing a club to his partner's ten. West also had the ten of diamonds to cash; two down.

In Pairs events it is just as important to save overtricks as to beat contracts.

Game All. Dealer North.

        ♠ Q
        ♡ 109653
        ◇ 7532
        ♣ K62

♠ 10873
♡ KQ742
◇ A84
♣ J

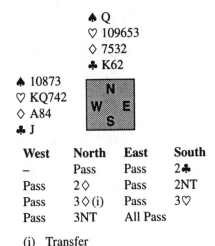

West	North	East	South
–	Pass	Pass	2♣
Pass	2◇	Pass	2NT
Pass	3◇(i)	Pass	3♡
Pass	3NT	All Pass	

(i) Transfer

You start off with the three of spades against South's three no trumps. The queen holds in dummy and declarer plays a diamond to partner's six and his nine. Plan the defence.

Gather the evidence: Declarer has shown 23-24 HCP and dummy has 5, leaving very few for partner. However, the cards do not seem to be lying very well for declarer. It is unlikely that he will be able to use dummy's hearts. Hopefully partner will have just enough in clubs to stop declarer making too many tricks in the suit. The diamond position is very unclear.

Make a plan: Whatever the diamond position is, it looks as if declarer has guessed well. Some possibilities are four-card suits QJ109, KJ109, Q109x, K109x; of course he may only have three cards – QJ9, KJ9, Q109, K109. In none of these situations does it seem to be advantageous to win the ace. If you duck smoothly it will serve two purposes: firstly, declarer will not know the diamond position either and that must be to your advantage; secondly, you will find out more about the hand and will be more likely to find the right defence when you do get the lead.

Implement the plan: Play the four of diamonds. The full deal:

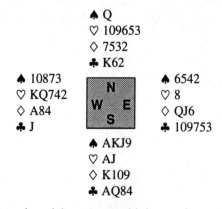

```
                    ♠ Q
                    ♡ 109653
                    ◊ 7532
                    ♣ K62
   ♠ 10873                        ♠ 6542
   ♡ KQ742                        ♡ 8
   ◊ A84                          ◊ QJ6
   ♣ J                            ♣ 109753
                    ♠ AKJ9
                    ♡ AJ
                    ◊ K109
                    ♣ AQ84
```

Declarer now has nine tricks on top and it is true that he can still make a tenth if he plays the king of diamonds from hand as West cannot attack hearts to advantage. However, he hadn't a clue how the diamond suit was divided – perhaps East had AQJxx – so he cashed his tricks, hoping that clubs would provide him with a tenth trick.

Love All. Dealer South.

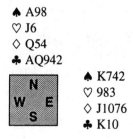

```
                    ♠ A98
                    ♡ J6
                    ◊ Q54
                    ♣ AQ942
                                 ♠ K742
                                 ♡ 983
                                 ◊ J1076
                                 ♣ K10
```

West	North	East	South
–	–	–	1NT
Pass	3NT	All Pass	

Your partner leads the four of hearts against South's three no trumps. Declarer wins the jack in dummy and plays the two of clubs. Plan the defence.

Gather the evidence: Dummy does not have a lot to spare for his raise to three no trumps so declarer might struggle if you defend passively. On the other hand, it does not look as if partner has found a sparkling opening lead.

Make a plan: If you play the king of clubs you can see that declarer will make at least three tricks in the suit. There are two more in dummy (ace of spades and jack of hearts). Surely he can make four in his hand. There must be more chances if you don't play the king of clubs.

Implement the plan: Play the ten of clubs. The full deal:

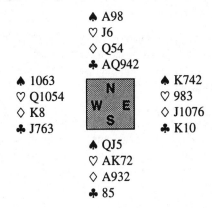

```
                    ♠ A98
                    ♡ J6
                    ◇ Q54
                    ♣ AQ942
    ♠ 1063                        ♠ K742
    ♡ Q1054          N            ♡ 983
    ◇ K8         W       E        ◇ J1076
    ♣ J763           S            ♣ K10
                    ♠ QJ5
                    ♡ AK72
                    ◇ A932
                    ♣ 85
```

Of course, you were presented with the problem at the wrong place. If you had taken the time to think it all through, declarer would have never gone wrong in the club suit. You should have done your thinking at trick one.

This deal comes from 1995 European Championship. Germany's Klaus Reps was South and France's Michel Perron East. Perron played the ten of clubs without a flicker. When it held the trick he continued hearts. Reps won with the ace and took a long time before eventually playing a club to the queen. He could no longer recover.

I am sure Michel Perron had no clear plan when he played the ten of clubs. He just knew that partner's lead had not been a success and that declarer would probably make his contract if he had three club tricks.

2. Coups

Game All. Dealer East.

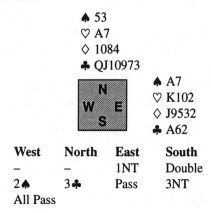

♠ 53
♡ A7
◇ 1084
♣ QJ10973

♠ A7
♡ K102
◇ J9532
♣ A62

West	North	East	South
–	–	1NT	Double
2♠	3♣	Pass	3NT
All Pass			

West leads the jack of spades to your ace and declarer's six. Plan the defence.

Gather the evidence: Partner surely has little in high cards and it is going to be up to you to beat South's three no trumps. Declarer is likely to hold the king of clubs, probably not singleton, and so is threatening to make a large number of tricks in dummy.

Make a plan: While you are not in a position to count defensive tricks, it would surely be to your side's advantage to reduce dummy's trick-taking potential. If you can remove the heart entry and then duck your ace of clubs until South runs out of the suit you should be able to minimise dummy's tricks. Then you can concentrate on trying to take five tricks.

Implement the plan: Play the king of hearts. The full deal:

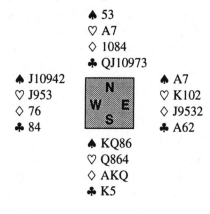

♠ 53
♡ A7
◇ 1084
♣ QJ10973

♠ J10942
♡ J953
◇ 76
♣ 84

♠ A7
♡ K102
◇ J9532
♣ A62

♠ KQ86
♡ Q864
◇ AKQ
♣ K5

Had you returned any other card at trick two declarer would have knocked out your ace of clubs and made eleven tricks – five clubs, three diamonds, a heart and two spades. As it was he was restricted to one club winner to go with two spades, two hearts and three diamonds – eight tricks only.

This deliberate sacrifice of an honour with the purpose of knocking out one of dummy's entries is known as a Merrimac Coup. The *Merrimac* was an Americal coal-carrying ship that was scuttled in Santiago harbour at the end of the nineteenth century in an effort to bottle up the Spanish fleet.

North/South Game. Dealer South.

♠ A10
♡ J2
◊ QJ1092
♣ QJ63

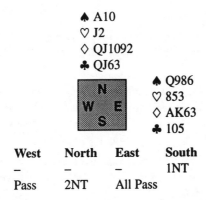

♠ Q986
♡ 853
◊ AK63
♣ 105

West	North	East	South
–	–	–	1NT
Pass	2NT	All Pass	

Your partner leads the king of hearts against two no trumps. He follows with the queen and ten, declarer winning the third round. Declarer now plays a diamond to dummy's queen. Plan the defence.

Gather the evidence: It is not clear whether partner began life with four or five hearts but it will not matter unless he gets the lead. His play in the suit (the ten of hearts) suggests his outside honour is in spades rather than clubs.

Make a plan: To beat 2NT you need an entry to partner's hand so he can cash his long heart. If you lead a low spade, unless partner has both the king and the jack, his king will force dummy's ace and his only remaining possible entry will have disappeared. If, on the other hand, you play the queen of spades you will create the required entry.

Implement the plan: Win the king of diamonds and play the queen of spades. The full deal:

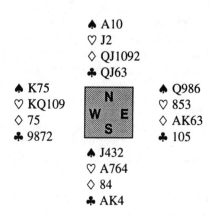

♠ A10
♡ J2
◇ QJ1092
♣ QJ63

♠ K75
♡ KQ109
◇ 75
♣ 9872

♠ Q986
♡ 853
◇ AK63
♣ 105

♠ J432
♡ A764
◇ 84
♣ AK4

Note that declarer was helpless after your switch to the queen of spades. If he ducks you continue the suit and either way you will be able to put partner in with the king of spades when you get in with your second diamond honour.

This play is very similar to the Merrimac Coup described above, but it is concerned with creating an entry to partner's hand rather than destroying the entry to one of declarer's. It is known as a Deschapelles Coup.

There are many hands written up that involve declarer squeezing either or both opponents. It is much rarer for the defenders to have the opportunity to squeeze declarer.

North/South Game. Dealer West.

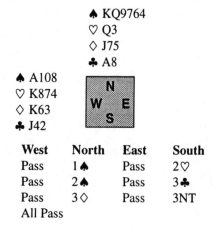

♠ KQ9764
♡ Q3
◇ J75
♣ A8

♠ A108
♡ K874
◇ K63
♣ J42

West	North	East	South
Pass	1♠	Pass	2♡
Pass	2♠	Pass	3♣
Pass	3◇	Pass	3NT
All Pass			

With a difficult choice, you lead the three of diamonds against South's three no trumps. This trick goes five, nine, queen. Declarer now plays a heart to dummy's queen, a heart to his ace and a third heart, partner turning up with J9 doubleton. You switch to a club. Declarer wins with dummy's ace and plays a second club to his ten and your jack, partner following upwards. What now?

Gather the evidence: This has really turned into a double-dummy problem. Declarer is known to have ♡A10xxx, ◊AQx and ♣K10xxx.

Make a plan: It looks as if declarer has made his contract. He is threatening to take three hearts, two diamonds and four clubs and all you can see is a spade, two hearts and a club. If you return, say, a club he will win, concede a heart and claim nine tricks. However, look at the effect of cashing your ace of spades. What can declarer discard? If he throws a diamond you can exit with a diamond and have the king to cash when you get in with the king of hearts; if he doesn't throw a diamond he must throw a winner and you can exit with a club, having first cashed the king of hearts.

Implement the plan: Cash the ace of spades. The full deal:

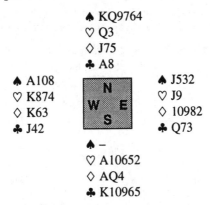

```
              ♠ KQ9764
              ♡ Q3
              ◊ J75
              ♣ A8
 ♠ A108                      ♠ J532
 ♡ K874         N            ♡ J9
 ◊ K63       W     E         ◊ 10982
 ♣ J42          S            ♣ Q73
              ♠ -
              ♡ A10652
              ◊ AQ4
              ♣ K10965
```

Declarer would have done better to play clubs after the queen of hearts held in dummy. But that is no excuse for misdefending.

North/South Game. Dealer South.

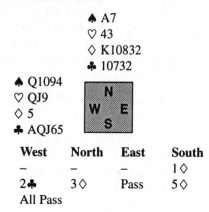

	♠ A7
	♡ 43
	◊ K10832
	♣ 10732

♠ Q1094
♡ QJ9
◊ 5
♣ AQJ65

West	North	East	South
–	–	–	1◊
2♣	3◊	Pass	5◊
All Pass			

You lead the queen of hearts which declarer wins in hand with the king, partner playing the two. Declarer draws two rounds of trumps, partner following, cashes the ace of hearts, ruffs a heart in dummy, cashes the ace of spades and plays a spade to his king, partner following with the two and the three. Now declarer plays the nine of clubs from hand. Plan the defence.

Gather the evidence: You need to take three club tricks to beat five diamonds. It looks as if declarer has eliminated both major suits.

Make a plan: Partner has a singleton club and declarer three. If partner's club is a small one there is nothing to be done; you will win your jack and give declarer a trick with his king. However, if partner's club is the king and you rise with the ace, you will then be able to cash two more club tricks.

Implement the plan: Play the ace of clubs. The full deal:

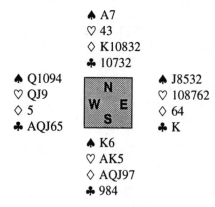

	♠ A7	
	♡ 43	
	◊ K10832	
	♣ 10732	

♠ Q1094   ♠ J8532
♡ QJ9   ♡ 108762
◊ 5   ◊ 64
♣ AQJ65   ♣ K

        ♠ K6
        ♡ AK5
        ◊ AQJ97
        ♣ 984

This is known as a Crocodile Coup. The West hand must open its jaws with the ace of clubs, gobbling up partner's king.

Note that we had to assume partner had the king of clubs or the contract would have been laydown and we must assume the contract can be beaten. Of course, in this instance, declarer's bidding would have been even more eccentric than it was had he held the king of clubs in addition to his other values.

A Bath Coup, where declarer ducks the opening lead of the king when he has AJx, is one that is more commonly seen in the context of declarer play, though it can turn up in defence. This is a variation on that theme.

Game All. Dealer South.

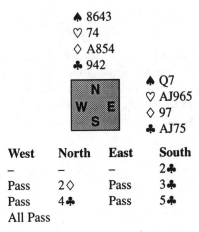

```
              ♠ 8643
              ♡ 74
              ◇ A854
              ♣ 942
                            ♠ Q7
                            ♡ AJ965
                            ◇ 97
                            ♣ AJ75
```

West	North	East	South
–	–	–	2♣
Pass	2◇	Pass	3♣
Pass	4♣	Pass	5♣
All Pass			

Your partner leads the two of hearts to your ace, declarer playing the three. You return a heart to declarer's king, partner playing the eight. Declarer lays down the king of clubs on which partner discards the two of spades. Plan the defence.

Gather the evidence: It is unlikely that you have any defensive tricks outside the trump suit, but it does look as if you have two trump tricks so you need to make sure that they don't disappear.

Make a plan: Declarer's trump holding is KQ10863. If you win the king of clubs he will cross to the ace of diamonds and run the nine of clubs, then a small club and that will pick up your remaining J75. On the other hand, if you duck the king of clubs, when he crosses to the ace of diamonds and plays a second club you will rise with the ace and make a further trick with your jack later in the play.

Implement the plan: Play the five of clubs. The full deal:

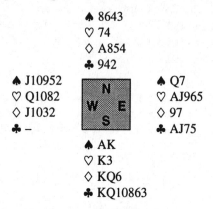

```
                    ♠ 8643
                    ♡ 74
                    ◊ A854
                    ♣ 942
    ♠ J10952                      ♠ Q7
    ♡ Q1082          N            ♡ AJ965
    ◊ J1032      W       E        ◊ 97
    ♣ –              S            ♣ AJ75
                    ♠ AK
                    ♡ K3
                    ◊ KQ6
                    ♣ KQ10863
```

The hands we have seen in this section are not very common but they do crop up from time to time. Although they are spectacular they do not account for anything like as many lost IMPs as the more run-of-the-mill hands where the general principles of counting and communications and thinking logically will stand you in good stead.

3. Specific card chosen

Consider the following layout:

```
            10xx
    Axx             KJ9x
            Qxx
```

If you, East, decide to switch to this suit you must play the jack. If you play low, declarer can duck to your partner's ace and later make a trick with his queen. If you switch to the jack he has no such chance.

```
            9xx
    Kxx             Q1087
            AJx
```

Similarly, if as East you play this suit you must play the ten, forcing declarer to play an honour. If you play small, he will duck to your partner's king and he will later be able to pick up your queen.

Of course, when experts play experts anything can happen. The following hand occurred in the 1995 US Nationals which were played in New Orleans:

Game All. Dealer West.

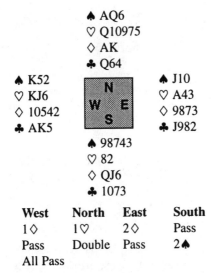

```
                    ♠ AQ6
                    ♡ Q10975
                    ◇ AK
                    ♣ Q64
     ♠ K52                           ♠ J10
     ♡ KJ6            N              ♡ A43
     ◇ 10542       W     E           ◇ 9873
     ♣ AK5            S              ♣ J982
                    ♠ 98743
                    ♡ 82
                    ◇ QJ6
                    ♣ 1073
```

West	North	East	South
1◇	1♡	2◇	Pass
Pass	Double	Pass	2♠
All Pass			

The two experts in question were West, Brian Glubok, and South, Ed Nagy. West did well with his choice of opening lead, selecting a passive diamond rather than his ace-king of clubs. Declarer cashed the two top diamonds and led a heart to West's jack. West switched to a low club, confident that declarer would not place him with the ace and king because of his failure to lead the suit at trick one. However, declarer called for dummy's queen and soon made his contract. The reason he made the successful play in the club suit was that he 'knew' that West would have switched to the jack of clubs from AJx or KJx. The play of the queen was his only chance of success.

We have spoken already about the useful advice contained in the BOLS tips. In the first year of the competition, the late Rixi Markus offered the following piece of advice: when, as a defender, you are about to attack from a holding such as Jx, Qx or Kx, consider the possible advantage of leading a low card. The hand that Rixi used to illustrate her tip was the following:

Love All. Dealer South.

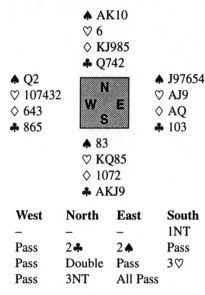

♠ AK10
♡ 6
◇ KJ985
♣ Q742

♠ Q2
♡ 107432
◇ 643
♣ 865

♠ J97654
♡ AJ9
◇ AQ
♣ 103

♠ 83
♡ KQ85
◇ 1072
♣ AKJ9

West	North	East	South
–	–	–	1NT
Pass	2♣	2♠	Pass
Pass	Double	Pass	3♡
Pass	3NT	All Pass	

As South was unwilling to pass his partner's penalty double of two spades, it seemed clear that the spade strength was likely to be in the dummy. Accordingly, in view of the absence of any re-entry Rixi decided to lead the two of spades rather than the queen.

As you can see, declarer could no longer cope with his task. He won with the ace, entered his hand with a club, and led a diamond, losing to East's queen. Declarer ducked the spade return, allowing the queen to hold, but West was able to put her partner in with the ace of hearts to clear the spades. Now South could take only eight tricks.

It is easy to see that if West leads the queen of spades initially, declarer will win with the ace and make the contract, as East will be unable to attack spades effectively.

There are other situations where leading low from honour doubleton proves to be the successful defence. The following deal features World Junior Champion, Tom Townsend, playing in a Pairs qualifying round in an American National.

Game All. Dealer North.

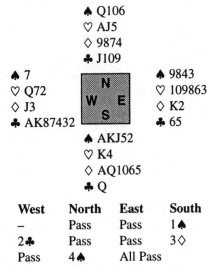

♠ Q106
♡ AJ5
◇ 9874
♣ J109

♠ 7
♡ Q72
◇ J3
♣ AK87432

♠ 9843
♡ 109863
◇ K2
♣ 65

♠ AKJ52
♡ K4
◇ AQ1065
♣ Q

West	North	East	South
–	Pass	Pass	1♠
2♣	Pass	Pass	3◇
Pass	4♠	All Pass	

He led the king of clubs and had the problem of what to switch to at trick two. Most Wests switched to a heart and declarer made twelve tricks with no difficulty. Tom did rather better by switching to the three of diamonds. Declarer won East's king with his ace, drew trumps, played a heart to dummy and played a diamond to ... his ten.

Note that West's jack may well have scored even if partner's king of diamonds had been the queen.

East/West Game. Dealer East.

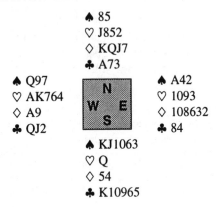

♠ 85
♡ J852
◇ KQJ7
♣ A73

♠ Q97
♡ AK764
◇ A9
♣ QJ2

♠ A42
♡ 1093
◇ 108632
♣ 84

♠ KJ1063
♡ Q
◇ 54
♣ K10965

West	North	East	South
–	–	Pass	Pass
1♡	Pass	Pass	1♠
Pass	1NT	Pass	2♣
Pass	2♠	All Pass	

South's two spades looks fairly secure, with declarer expecting to lose one trick in each side suit and two trump tricks. West led the ace of hearts and switched to the nine of diamonds! Declarer won the king in dummy and played a spade to the jack and queen. West continued his deception by switching to the jack of clubs. Declarer won the ace, took a club finesse ... and the roof fell in. West cashed the ace of diamonds, gave his partner a club ruff and then a diamond back promoted West's nine of spades. Two down.

4.   Attack communications

Game All. Dealer South.

♠ J5
♡ 653
◇ AKQ94
♣ 1053

♠ Q10842
♡ J8
◇ J6
♣ J864

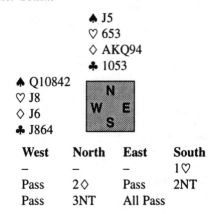

West	North	East	South
–	–	–	1♡
Pass	2◇	Pass	2NT
Pass	3NT	All Pass	

You lead the four of spades against South's three no trumps. Partner wins the ace and returns the seven to your queen. Declarer wins the third round with the king, partner following with the six. Declarer now plays a diamond. Plan the defence.

Gather the evidence: You have two more spade tricks to cash if you could ever get the lead. This looks unlikely. Declarer is obviously hoping to make some diamond tricks in the dummy.

Make a plan: If declarer has three or more diamonds, the situation looks hopeless. With five diamond tricks and one spade, declarer can surely manage three more from hearts and clubs with any honours partner may have well placed for declarer. You must hope declarer has only two diamonds. If he needs only four diamond tricks, he is probably planning to duck one round of the suit. You can stop him doing this by playing the jack as he cannot afford your hand to get the lead. This will restrict him to only three tricks in the suit and may leave him a trick short.

Implement the plan: Play the jack of diamonds. The full deal:

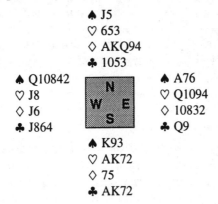

```
                    ♠ J5
                    ♡ 653
                    ◊ AKQ94
                    ♣ 1053
  ♠ Q10842                          ♠ A76
  ♡ J8                              ♡ Q1094
  ◊ J6                              ◊ 10832
  ♣ J864                            ♣ Q9
                    ♠ K93
                    ♡ AK72
                    ◊ 75
                    ♣ AK72
```

Declarer can still succeed in his contract if he reads the distribution perfectly. He can cash one more top diamond and then cash the aces and kings of hearts and clubs before exiting with a heart. That way your partner will be endplayed into giving him an extra diamond trick at the end. But why should declarer find that line of play? He would go down in a very straightforward contract if you had played the jack of diamonds from J10x.

Game All. Dealer South.

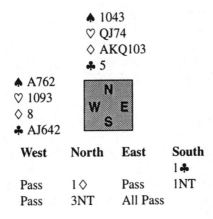

```
                    ♠ 1043
                    ♡ QJ74
                    ◊ AKQ103
                    ♣ 5
  ♠ A762
  ♡ 1093
  ◊ 8
  ♣ AJ642
```

West	North	East	South
			1♣
Pass	1◊	Pass	1NT
Pass	3NT	All Pass	

Not fancying a lead in declarer's bid suit, you choose instead the nine of hearts. Declarer wins in hand with the ace, your partner playing the two, and cashes the ace and king of diamonds, your partner playing the two and five. Declarer now plays a club to partner's three, his king and your ace. Plan the defence?

Gather the evidence: It looks as if declarer has AKx in hearts. Presumably he has at least five clubs since he did not open or rebid a four-card major and has only two diamonds. Declarer cannot have KQ10987 of clubs or he would have played a top club at trick two. This would have set up his eighth trick immediately; then, assuming he has at least one spade stopper, either you give him a spade for his ninth trick, or you play something else and he can set up more club tricks. Therefore declarer has ♣KQ987 (your partner would fail to peter only if he had a club honour). You can virtually write down his hand: ♠K(orQ)Jx ♡AKx ◇xx ♣KQ987.

Make a plan: You cannot prevent declarer from establishing nine tricks (a spade, four hearts, three diamonds and a club) before you have five but what you can do is prevent him from getting at them all. The only suit in which he has any communication is hearts so that is the suit that you must play.

Implement the plan: Continue with the ten of hearts. The full deal:

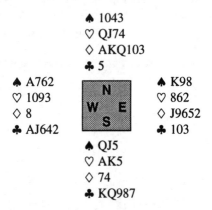

```
                ♠ 1043
                ♡ QJ74
                ◇ AKQ103
                ♣ 5
  ♠ A762                    ♠ K98
  ♡ 1093           N        ♡ 862
  ◇ 8          W     E      ◇ J9652
  ♣ AJ642          S        ♣ 103
                ♠ QJ5
                ♡ AK5
                ◇ 74
                ♣ KQ987
```

Do you see what a problem you have given declarer? Suppose he wins the heart in hand and plays the queen of spades. You hop up with the ace and play a third heart. Declarer can cash his two heart tricks but now what? He cannot cash the queen of diamonds or your partner will be able to take the setting trick in that suit when he gets in with the king of spades. So declarer plays a second spade immediately. Now your partner rises with the king and plays a third spade. Declarer is stuck in hand with only clubs left. When he concedes a trick to your jack of clubs you will cash a long spade.

There are other variations where declarer wins the second heart in the North hand but there is no way he can arrive at all of his tricks.

This all sounds very complicated and you may be thinking that you would never be able to work all this out at the table. Neither can the expert. But what he would work out is that declarer had nine tricks coming to him before you could arrive at five. Therefore the only hope was to sever his communications and that the best way to do that is usually to play on declarer's most flexible suit.

Sometimes a ruff and discard is the way to tangle declarer's communications, especially if partner is also void in the suit played.

East/West Game. Dealer East.

♠ K93
♡ 10762
◇ 3
♣ A9743

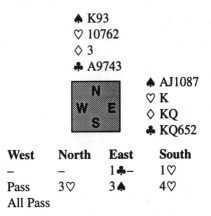

♠ AJ1087
♡ K
◇ KQ
♣ KQ652

West	North	East	South
–	–	1♣–	1♡
Pass	3♡	3♠	4♡
All Pass			

Your partner leads the queen of spades against South's four hearts. When it holds he continues with another spade to your jack and the ace of spades on which he discards the jack of clubs. Plan the defence.

Gather the evidence: If partner had a singleton club he would surely have led it after we had opened the suit. South must have the ace of diamonds for his four heart bid. The most likely source of a further trick is the trump suit.

Make a plan: A fourth round of spades may succeed in one of two ways: either it may promote partner's Jx of trumps; or it will allow him to pitch his remaining club which may be embarrassing for declarer.

Implement the plan: Play the ten of spades. The full deal:

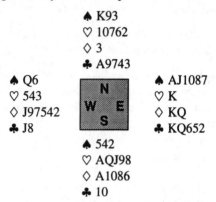

```
            ♠ K93
            ♡ 10762
            ◊ 3
            ♣ A9743
♠ Q6                      ♠ AJ1087
♡ 543         N           ♡ K
◊ J97542   W     E        ◊ KQ
♣ J8          S           ♣ KQ652
            ♠ 542
            ♡ AQJ98
            ◊ A1086
            ♣ 10
```

Once West threw his second club, declarer could never make a club trick without drawing trumps and therefore ruining his cross-ruff.

North/South Game. Dealer South.

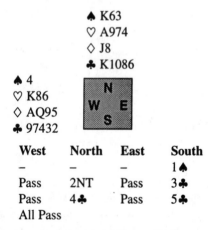

```
            ♠ K63
            ♡ A974
            ◊ J8
            ♣ K1086
♠ 4
♡ K86         N
◊ AQ95     W     E
♣ 97432       S
```

West	North	East	South
–	–	–	1♠
Pass	2NT	Pass	3♣
Pass	4♣	Pass	5♣
All Pass			

Against five clubs you lead the ace of diamonds followed by the queen of diamonds, declarer ruffing the second. He lays down the ace of clubs on which your partner, not surprisingly, discards a diamond, then cashes the ace of spades, plays a spade to the king (partner petering) and a third spade to his ten. You ruff and exit with a club which declarer wins in hand to play the queen of hearts. Can you beat this game?

Gather the evidence: You already know declarer's holdings in the minor suits and it looks as if he has ♠AQ10xx.

Make a plan: For declarer's spade suit to be of any use to him, he needs an entry to it after he has drawn trumps. That entry can only be the jack of hearts which will not be an entry unless you cover the queen of hearts.

Implement the plan: Play the six of hearts. The full deal:

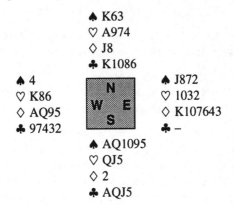

```
              ♠ K63
              ♡ A974
              ◊ J8
              ♣ K1086
♠ 4                           ♠ J872
♡ K86                         ♡ 1032
◊ AQ95                        ◊ K107643
♣ 97432                       ♣ -
              ♠ AQ1095
              ♡ QJ5
              ◊ 2
              ♣ AQJ5
```

This was one of Italy's successful boards in their match against Great Britain in the 1995 European Championship (though on a different bidding sequence). West somewhat lazily covered the queen of hearts. Declarer won with the ace, drew trumps and crossed back to the jack of hearts to cash his good spades. In the other room the British pair bid to the rather more normal contract of four spades where an initial club lead, ruffed by East, a diamond return and second club ruff meant declarer had to go one down because of the unavoidable heart loser.

Of course, you do not always need to establish communications. Sometimes you can try so hard to give partner the lead that you can overlook the obvious.

Game All. Dealer East.

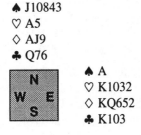

```
              ♠ J10843
              ♡ A5
              ◊ AJ9
              ♣ Q76
                              ♠ A
                              ♡ K1032
                              ◊ KQ652
                              ♣ K103
```

West	North	East	South
–	–	1◊	1♠
Pass	3◊(i)	Pass	4♠
All Pass			

(i) High-card raise to 3♠ or better

Your partner leads the eight of diamonds against South's four spades. Declarer plays dummy's nine and you win with the queen. Plan the defence.

Gather the evidence: It cannot be realistic to expect any help from partner in terms of defensive tricks. You must look to your own hand. It looks as if partner has led a doubleton diamond (or just possibly a singleton).

Make a plan: Provided partner has a doubleton spade, you can see a sure way to beat four spades. If you return a diamond now, sacrificing your second trick in the suit you will be able to give partner a ruff when you get in with the ace of spades. You can see that there is no way for declarer to get rid of a diamond loser in time. Then, in the fullness of time, you will make your king of hearts. Of course, it is possible that you can defeat the contract in a different way, perhaps by taking two diamonds and a heart to go with your ace of trumps, but it is better to go for the sure thing.

Implement the plan: Play the six of diamonds. The full deal:

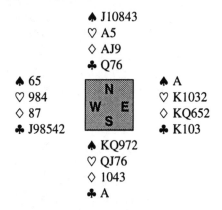

```
            ♠ J10843
            ♡ A5
            ◊ AJ9
            ♣ Q76
♠ 65                        ♠ A
♡ 984                       ♡ K1032
◊ 87                        ◊ KQ652
♣ J98542                    ♣ K103
            ♠ KQ972
            ♡ QJ76
            ◊ 1043
            ♣ A
```

The six of diamonds was a suit-preference signal, asking partner to play a heart when he next gets the lead. When you actually give him his ruff a couple of tricks later, you can play the king of diamonds and he should get the message, not that it matters unduly on this occasion.

5. Avoiding the squeeze/endplay

Game All. Dealer North.

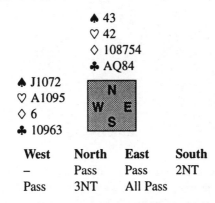

```
                ♠ 43
                ♡ 42
                ◊ 108754
                ♣ AQ84
    ♠ J1072        
    ♡ A1095      N
    ◊ 6        W     E
    ♣ 10963       S
```

West	North	East	South
–	Pass	Pass	2NT
Pass	3NT	All Pass	

You make the aggressive lead of the ten of hearts which partner wins with the queen. He returns the three of hearts to declarer's jack and your ace. Plan the defence.

Gather the evidence: It looks as if partner started with ♡KQxx (with KQx he would have cashed the king; with ♡KQxxx he would have returned his fourth highest). You could cash two more heart tricks but it seems unlikely that your partner holds an ace. You must hope that he can stop the run of the diamond suit to have any chances.

Make a plan: If partner can stop the run of the diamond suit he really needs Qxx (J9xx is a possibility). When declarer cashes the ace and king of diamonds what are you going to discard? A club is very likely to give him a long trick in the suit (unless he had four tricks in any event). A spade discard will also be good for declarer whenever he has four cards in the suit. There is no need to cash hearts now as partner can do that later, after winning his diamond trick. It looks best to get off play in a black suit.

Implement the plan: Play the jack of spades. The full deal:

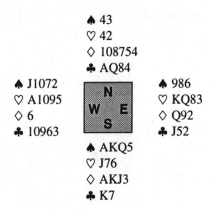

♠ 43
♡ 42
◇ 108754
♣ AQ84

♠ J1072   ♠ 986
♡ A1095   ♡ KQ83
◇ 6   ◇ Q92
♣ 10963   ♣ J52

♠ AKQ5
♡ J76
◇ AKJ3
♣ K7

Had you continued to cash your heart winners you would have been squeezed when declarer cashed his second top diamond. Now you have given him a chance to go wrong. Obviously he might guess diamonds correctly, but if he cashes the ace and king you can throw a heart and he is down. If he plays another diamond your partner will cash two hearts; if he doesn't he has no chance of establishing a ninth winner.

The following was a three-stage problem and no defenders succeeded in the 1994 Junior European Championship.

Love All. Dealer South.

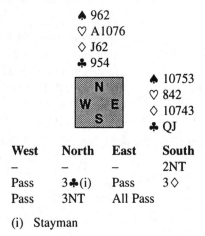

♠ 962
♡ A1076
◇ J62
♣ 954

♠ 10753
♡ 842
◇ 10743
♣ QJ

West	North	East	South
–	–	–	2NT
Pass	3♣(i)	Pass	3◇
Pass	3NT	All Pass	

(i) Stayman

Your partner leads the four of spades against South's three no trumps. Dummy plays the two. Plan the defence.

Gather the evidence: Partner has led from a four-card spade suit.

Make a plan: If he had three of the top four honours he would surely have led one of them. This marks declarer with two honours doubleton. In this case there is no need to play your ten which may come in useful later as an entry.

Implement the plan: Play the seven of spades to show an even number.

Declarer wins with the queen and plays ace, king and another club. Partner plays the three, the eight and then the ten. What do you discard?

Gather the evidence: Declarer has four club tricks, one (at least) spade and one heart. It is very likely that partner has honours in each red suit.

Make a plan: You know that he can safely play another spade, the ace if he has it. Partner also knows this because he knows you have four spades as your seven could not be from a doubleton (declarer has denied four). Your ten of diamonds will only be a trick if declarer has AKxx, unlikely since he has already shown up with five clubs. Indeed, if he does have AKxx in diamonds he has nine tricks.

Implement the plan: Discard the seven of diamonds.

Partner cashes the ace of spades, declarer's king dropping, and continues with the jack of spades and then the eight to your ten, declarer discarding the three of hearts and five of diamonds. What now?

Gather the evidence: If partner had the ace of diamonds he would surely have cashed it.

Make a plan: Declarer has lost four tricks so an endplay is out of the question. If you need to break up a squeeze, it must be right to play a heart, trying to sever declarer's communications. If you can knock out his only entry to dummy, all his legitimate squeeze chances will disappear. The only risk attached to switching to a heart is that he might have KJx and need a heart guess for his contract, however that cannot be so as he has discarded a low heart.

Implement the plan: Play the eight of hearts. The full deal:

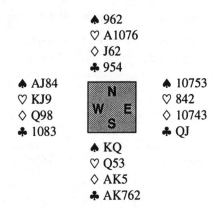

♠ 962
♡ A1076
◇ J62
♣ 954

♠ AJ84
♡ KJ9
◇ Q98
♣ 1083

♠ 10753
♡ 842
◇ 10743
♣ QJ

♠ KQ
♡ Q53
◇ AK5
♣ AK762

Declarer now has no chance. The eight of hearts will probably be covered by the queen, king and ace. Declarer will cross back to his hand with a diamond and run his clubs. Partner will have no difficulty in hanging on to his jack of hearts.

There were a number of hurdles to overcome on this deal. Firstly, you had to refrain from playing your ten of spades at trick one. Secondly, you had to discard a red suit on the third club. Suppose you had discarded a spade. Now partner would have cashed the ace of spades, played a spade to your ten and you would have tried to break up the squeeze with a heart. The heart would have gone to the queen, king and ace, say. Declarer would have come back to hand with a diamond and run his clubs. His last three cards would be a heart and ◇K5. Your partner would have to find a discard from ♡J9 and ◇Q9 (his master spade would have gone on the previous trick). If he threw a heart declarer would have exited in the suit, forcing him to lead a diamond; if he threw a diamond declarer would have dropped his queen.

5
LOSING OPTIONS

We saw in the Introduction the wonderfully deceptive defence that won a brilliancy prize for Gabriel Chagas. Possibly the greatest 'defence that never was' occurred in the last set of a closely fought Bermuda Bowl final.

North/South Game. Dealer East.

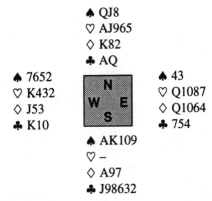

```
                ♠ QJ8
                ♡ AJ965
                ◇ K82
                ♣ AQ
   ♠ 7652                    ♠ 43
   ♡ K432        N           ♡ Q1087
   ◇ J53      W     E        ◇ Q1064
   ♣ K10         S           ♣ 754
                ♠ AK109
                ♡ –
                ◇ A97
                ♣ J98632
```

The 1975 Bermuda Bowl was coming to an end but there was very little dividing the two teams. Belladonna and Garozzo (South and North respectively) had had a long, artificial auction to seven clubs. West, Eddie Kantar, feeling quite confident because he expected the ace of clubs to be in declarer's hand, led a heart. Declarer ruffed in hand and had little to do but play on trumps. He led to the queen, cashed the ace and made his grand slam.

Kantar missed a great opportunity. Suppose he had played the king of clubs at trick two. If Belladonna had taken this at face value he would still have had a genuine chance for his contract. Suppose East's hand had been:

```
                ♠ xxx
                ♡ xxxx
                ◇ xx
                ♣ 10754
```

Declarer cashes the ace of hearts discarding a diamond, ruffs a second heart, cashes the ace-king of diamonds and three rounds of spades ending in dummy. He now ruffs a heart and ruffs a spade with the queen of clubs. The lead is now in dummy and his J9 are poised over East's 107. This line of play only requires East to have at least three spades and at least two diamonds, quite a high probability. On this occasion it would not have worked because East would have ruffed the third round of spades. Declarer would then have been mortified to discover that he could simply have drawn trumps.

We will never know what Belladonna would have done.

The following is another attractive example of what can be achieved by a judicious falsecard:

Game All. Dealer West.

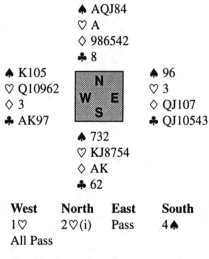

```
                ♠ AQJ84
                ♡ A
                ◇ 986542
                ♣ 8
  ♠ K105                        ♠ 96
  ♡ Q10962                      ♡ 3
  ◇ 3                           ◇ QJ107
  ♣ AK97                        ♣ QJ10543
                ♠ 732
                ♡ KJ8754
                ◇ AK
                ♣ 62
```

West	North	East	South
1♡	2♡(i)	Pass	4♠
All Pass			

(i)   Spades and a minor

Against South's four spades, West led the king of clubs and continued with a low heart to dummy's ace. Declarer played a diamond to hand and a spade to the queen. He now played a diamond back to hand and West ruffed with the king of spades! West continued with another heart and declarer discarded from dummy as he 'knew' that East had the ten and nine of spades left so that ruffing high would promote a trump trick. East ruffed with the spade nine and played another club which was ruffed on the table. Declarer now ruffed a diamond low in hand and West overruffed with the ten! One down.

The whole area of deceptive play is very difficult and one that needs to be treated with caution. Although we will begin with a look at areas where the intention is deliberately to deceive partner, all too often it is partner who is misled in our intent to deceive declarer. It is wisest to choose a moment when it is unlikely that partner will have little further to do with the defence. Of course, giving declarer a losing option does not always involve deception and we will look at examples towards the end of the chapter.

This chapter is divided into three sections:

1. Deceiving partner
2. Deceiving declarer
3. The losing option

1. Deceiving partner

You will be pleased to read that this is a short section. We would not like to ruin a beautiful friendship by too much deception!

The reason for sometimes trying to deceive partner is to force him to do the right thing when he might have had a losing alternative. Look at this example:

East/West Game. Dealer South.

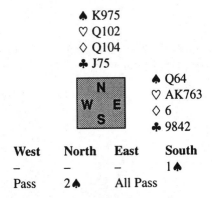

```
              ♠ K975
              ♡ Q102
              ◊ Q104
              ♣ J75
                              ♠ Q64
          N                   ♡ AK763
        W   E                 ◊ 6
          S                   ♣ 9842
```

West	North	East	South
–	–	–	1 ♠
Pass	2 ♠	All Pass	

Your partner leads the jack of hearts and declarer plays the queen from dummy. Plan the defence.

Gather the evidence: You can see three defensive tricks – two top hearts and a heart ruff. It is too early to say with any certainty where the other three might come from, but if partner had the ace of diamonds it would be easy.

Make a plan: With no rush to take the heart ruff it would seem a good idea to switch to a diamond in case partner has the ace. The trouble with this is that partner might not realise that you have a singleton diamond and he might duck the diamond – not a good idea on this occasion. If he thought you did not have both heart honours he might be more inclined to win the ace of diamonds.

Implement the plan: Win trick one with the *ace* of hearts and play the six of diamonds. With any luck partner will win with the ace and give you a ruff. Then you can cash the king of hearts and give him a heart ruff which is also an entry for him to give you another diamond ruff. The full deal:

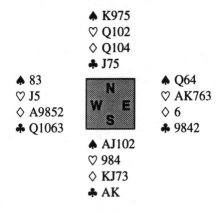

             ♠ K975
             ♡ Q102
             ◊ Q104
             ♣ J75

♠ 83   ♠ Q64
♡ J5   ♡ AK763
◊ A9852   ◊ 6
♣ Q1063   ♣ 9842

             ♠ AJ102
             ♡ 984
             ◊ KJ73
             ♣ AK

Sometimes partner's opening lead has been such a success that he might not believe it if you played true cards.

Game All. Dealer South.

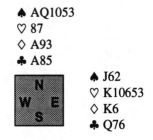

             ♠ AQ1053
             ♡ 87
             ◊ A93
             ♣ A85

                     ♠ J62
                     ♡ K10653
                     ◊ K6
                     ♣ Q76

West	North	East	South
–	–	–	1NT
Pass	2♡(i)	Pass	2♠
Pass	3NT	All Pass	

(i) Transfer to spades

Your partner leads the two of hearts to your king and declarer's four. Plan the defence.

Gather the evidence: What a clever partner! What a good lead! What can go wrong? If you quietly return your fourth highest heart, the five, declarer will play the queen and partner may go wrong. Don't forget that he has no room for an outside entry. From his point of view declarer may have Q1064 and you K53. If that is the case the only chance of four tricks in the suit is for him to switch and hope that you regain the lead to play another heart. He is particularly likely to go wrong because of the bidding. He will expect declarer to have a doubleton spade and will not expect him to have a doubleton heart as well.

Make a plan: He will be much less likely to go wrong if he thinks you have only four hearts. There will be no reason for him to switch because he will know his hearts are good.

Implement the plan: Return the three of hearts. The full deal:

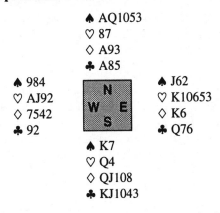

```
                    ♠ AQ1053
                    ♡ 87
                    ◇ A93
                    ♣ A85
    ♠ 984                           ♠ J62
    ♡ AJ92          N               ♡ K10653
    ◇ 7542      W       E           ◇ K6
    ♣ 92            S               ♣ Q76
                    ♠ K7
                    ♡ Q4
                    ◇ QJ108
                    ♣ KJ1043
```

On the other hand, if partner's lead has not been a success, we must be careful not to let him think that it has.

Love All. Dealer South.

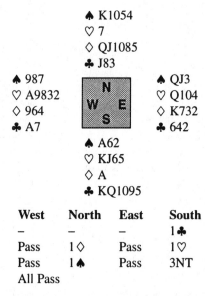

		♠ K1054	
		♡ 7	
		◇ QJ1085	
		♣ J83	

♠ 987		♠ QJ3
♡ A9832		♡ Q104
◇ 964		◇ K732
♣ A7		♣ 642

		♠ A62	
		♡ KJ65	
		◇ A	
		♣ KQ1095	

West	North	East	South
–	–	–	1♣
Pass	1◇	Pass	1♡
Pass	1♠	Pass	3NT
All Pass			

West led the eight of spades against South's no trump game. Suppose East plays the jack. Declarer will win with the ace and knock out West's ace of clubs. Will West not continue with another spade? Declarer will duck this and soon have nine tricks.

Suppose, on the other hand, East plays the queen of spades. Now when West gets in with the ace of clubs he will know that the spade suit offers little prospect and switch to a heart. East's queen will force the king and when East gets in with the jack of spades or king of diamonds he will be able to play the ten of hearts through declarer's holding and West will take four winners in the suit.

2.   Deceiving declarer

This section is best illustrated by some hands from actual play rather than a series of problems.

(a) leading a deceptive card

East/West Game. Dealer South.

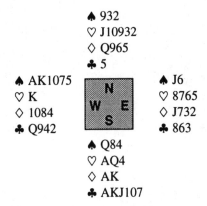

```
              ♠ 932
              ♡ J10932
              ◊ Q965
              ♣ 5
♠ AK1075                        ♠ J6
♡ K            N                ♡ 8765
◊ 1084      W     E             ◊ J732
♣ Q942         S               ♣ 863
              ♠ Q84
              ♡ AQ4
              ◊ AK
              ♣ AKJ107
```

This deal occurred in the final of the 1995 World Junior Championship. The British declarer in the Closed Room played in four hearts. He lost two top spades and a spade ruff and then had no reason not to take the heart finesse.

In the Open Room the New Zealanders reached three no trumps and it looked to the VuGraph audience that he would have to succeed. With the defenders threatening to take four spade tricks as soon as they got the lead he would have no option but to play both his long suits from the top and when the king of hearts dropped he would have ten tricks. However, Justin Hackett found the excellent opening lead of the five of spades. Now declarer thought it quite likely that spades were breaking 4-3. In which case he had a much better play for his game and that is what he tried. He played the queen of hearts, expecting it to hold the trick. Then he would revert to clubs. As long as spades were 4-3 he would make his contract whenever clubs were 4-3 or the queen dropped doubleton or the king of hearts was singleton or doubleton. Unfortunately for him Justin won his king of hearts and cashed *four* spade tricks.

(b) not winning a trick we could win easily

East/West Game. Dealer East.

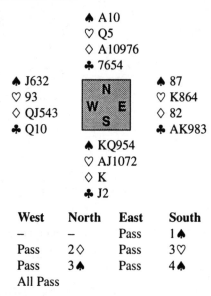

```
                  ♠ A10
                  ♡ Q5
                  ◊ A10976
                  ♣ 7654
   ♠ J632                        ♠ 87
   ♡ 93          N               ♡ K864
   ◊ QJ543   W       E           ◊ 82
   ♣ Q10         S               ♣ AK983
                  ♠ KQ954
                  ♡ AJ1072
                  ◊ K
                  ♣ J2
```

West	North	East	South
–	–	Pass	1♠
Pass	2◊	Pass	3♡
Pass	3♠	Pass	4♠
All Pass			

West opted to lead the unbid suit which turned out rather well. The queen of clubs held, so he continued with the ten of clubs to his partner's king. East continued with the eight of clubs which declarer ruffed with the nine.

Had West overruffed there would have been no further problems. Declarer would have won the trump continuation, taken a heart finesse, ruffed a heart in dummy, drawn trumps and claimed. However, this West smoothly discarded the nine of hearts.

Declarer was not sure of the heart finesse but he was sure of the spade position. He crossed to dummy with the ace of spades and ran the ten of spades. West won with the jack and there was now no way for declarer to avoid a heart loser.

It is surprising how a well-timed false card can put even an expert declarer off his stroke as the next hand illustrates.

Game All. Dealer South.

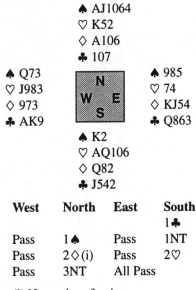

```
              ♠ AJ1064
              ♡ K52
              ◊ A106
              ♣ 107
  ♠ Q73                        ♠ 985
  ♡ J983                       ♡ 74
  ◊ 973                        ◊ KJ54
  ♣ AK9                        ♣ Q863
              ♠ K2
              ♡ AQ106
              ◊ Q82
              ♣ J542
```

West	North	East	South
			1♣
Pass	1♠	Pass	1NT
Pass	2◊(i)	Pass	2♡
Pass	3NT	All Pass	

(i) New minor forcing

This hand, reported by Alan Truscott in the *New York Times*, won the Precision Award for the Best Defence of 1995 for Zia Mahmood.

West led the three of diamonds (playing third and fifth) against South's three no trumps. Declarer played low from dummy and Zia played the *jack*. Obviously declarer could have played on spades but he decided to cash his red-suit winners. He saw the possibility of having seven red-suit winners which would be enough for his contract. Failing that, he would perhaps have put some pressure on his opponents and could exit in hearts, hoping to force an error in the endgame.

Declarer cashed three heart tricks and took a diamond finesse. Zia won and the defence soon took three clubs and a heart as well.

Matchpointed Pairs offers a great deal of scope for imaginative deception because declarer is always trying to make as many tricks as he can rather than simply trying to fulfil his contract. West's deception on the following deal would never have worked in a Team game.

Game All. Dealer East.

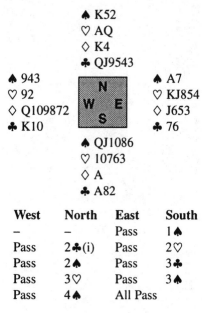

	♠ K52	
	♡ AQ	
	◇ K4	
	♣ QJ9543	

♠ 943		♠ A7
♡ 92		♡ KJ854
◇ Q109872		◇ J653
♣ K10		♣ 76

	♠ QJ1086	
	♡ 10763	
	◇ A	
	♣ A82	

West	North	East	South
–	–	Pass	1♠
Pass	2♣(i)	Pass	2♡
Pass	2♠	Pass	3♣
Pass	3♡	Pass	3♠
Pass	4♠	All Pass	

(i) Forcing to game

West, Paul Soloway, led the ten of diamonds which declarer won with the ace. He tried the queen of spades which East won with the ace and returned a second diamond. Declarer discarded a heart from hand and drew trumps. Now declarer ran the queen of clubs which held, West playing the ten. In a team game there would have been no further problem. Declarer would have guaranteed his contract by playing ace and another club, expecting simply to lose the king of clubs. However, not unreasonably, this declarer was greedy. He ran the jack of clubs to West's king. The club suit was now blocked and when West switched to a heart declarer had to lose two heart tricks to go with his two black-suit losers – one down.

Game All. Dealer South.

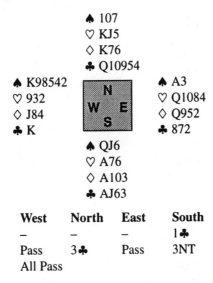

<pre>
                    ♠ 107
                    ♡ KJ5
                    ◊ K76
                    ♣ Q10954
      ♠ K98542   ♠ A3
      ♡ 932   N   ♡ Q1084
      ◊ J84   W   E   ◊ Q952
      ♣ K   S   ♣ 872
                    ♠ QJ6
                    ♡ A76
                    ◊ A103
                    ♣ AJ63
</pre>

West	North	East	South
–	–	–	1♣
Pass	3♣	Pass	3NT
All Pass			

West led the five of spades to his partner's ace and the three of spades was returned, declarer playing the jack. West ducked this trick, carefully playing the four. Look at this from declarer's point of view. He thought West had K9854 and East A32 so there was no reason for him to do other than cross to dummy and take the club finesse.

Now imagine that West had won the king of spades and cleared the suit. Declarer would have known that he could not afford to lose a trick to West so would have made the safety play of laying down the ace – not a play West wanted him to find!

(c)   playing an unnecessarily high card

Game All. Dealer West.

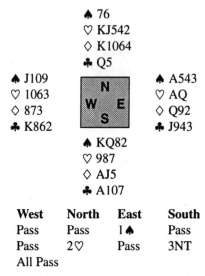

```
                    ♠ 76
                    ♡ KJ542
                    ◇ K1064
                    ♣ Q5
    ♠ J109                          ♠ A543
    ♡ 1063            N             ♡ AQ
    ◇ 873        W        E         ◇ Q92
    ♣ K862           S             ♣ J943
                    ♠ KQ82
                    ♡ 987
                    ◇ AJ5
                    ♣ A107
```

West	North	East	South
Pass	Pass	1 ♠	Pass
Pass	2 ♡	Pass	3NT
All Pass			

Against South's three no trumps, West led the jack of spades which ran round to declarer's queen. Declarer now ran the nine of hearts which East won with the ace! East continued with the ace of spades and a low spade. South, expecting East to have five spades for his opening bid, finessed the eight. West won the ten and exited with a club. Since West was known to have started with the jack of spades and queen of hearts there was no room for him to hold the king of clubs as well since he had passed East's opening bid, so declarer played low from dummy and East's jack forced the ace. Now a heart to the jack and queen and a club to West's king beat the contract by one trick.

The following deal was played in the 1995 European Championships and features Israel's Shalom Zeligman.

East/West Game. Dealer East.

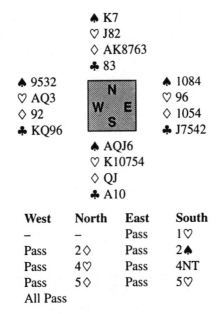

```
                    ♠ K7
                    ♡ J82
                    ◇ AK8763
                    ♣ 83
    ♠ 9532                        ♠ 1084
    ♡ AQ3            N            ♡ 96
    ◇ 92         W     E          ◇ 1054
    ♣ KQ96          S             ♣ J7542
                    ♠ AQJ6
                    ♡ K10754
                    ◇ QJ
                    ♣ A10
```

West	North	East	South
–	–	Pass	1♡
Pass	2◇	Pass	2♠
Pass	4♡	Pass	4NT
Pass	5◇	Pass	5♡
All Pass			

Although five hearts seems to be a level too high for safety, it has good chances as the cards lie. West, Zeligman, led the king of clubs. Declarer won and played three rounds of spades discarding a club. He then ruffed a club and led a low trump off the table. Had West won with the queen and played the fourth spade, declarer would have ruffed with the jack, come to hand with a diamond and played another heart. He would have had to guess whether to play the king to pin the nine, or small. Who knows whether or not he would have made his contract?

Zeligman found a better defence when he won the ten of hearts with the ace. Now when he returned the fourth round of spades, declarer could see no point in ruffing. He 'knew' East had the queen of hearts and would either have to ruff with it or would ruff with a small card that would mean his trump trick could be picked up next time. However, when East ruffed with the nine declarer had to go down.

It is not only winning a trick with an unnecessarily high honour that can work well, sometimes following suit can afford the same possibilities.

North/South Game. Dealer West.

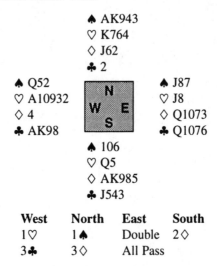

                    ♠ AK943
                    ♡ K764
                    ◊ J62
                    ♣ 2
    ♠ Q52   ♠ J87
    ♡ A10932   ♡ J8
    ◊ 4   ◊ Q1073
    ♣ AK98   ♣ Q1076
                    ♠ 106
                    ♡ Q5
                    ◊ AK985
                    ♣ J543

West	North	East	South
1♡	1♠	Double	2◊
3♣	3◊	All Pass	

This took place in a point-a-board event, i.e. a Teams event with Pairs scoring so overtricks and undertricks are very important. West led the king of clubs and continued the suit, dummy ruffing. Declarer now led the king of hearts, trying to set up a cross-ruff. West won and led a diamond. The six was played from dummy and East, Tony Forrester, played the queen! Declarer 'knew' that West had the ten of diamonds and, as he was already known to have five hearts and four clubs, there was a good chance that it would fall doubleton, so he cashed the other top diamond. Now he had to lose four tricks whereas his intended cross-ruff line would surely have netted ten.

(d) discarding

There is a great deal of skill needed to be a consistently good discarder. Most players content themselves with trying to help partner, taking care to describe their hand to him. Obviously one can give count by playing high-low from an even number (or an odd number if that is your preferred method) but the actual suit we discard from also gives a clue to our distribution – our first discard is usually from length, after all we do not want to make an early discard that might give declarer a trick or some vital clue about the hand. This is an area in which there is plenty of scope for deception.

North/South Game. Dealer South.

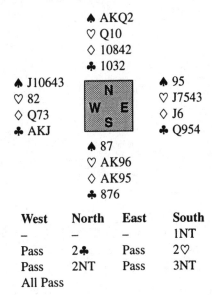

```
                  ♠ AKQ2
                  ♡ Q10
                  ◊ 10842
                  ♣ 1032
      ♠ J10643                      ♠ 95
      ♡ 82          N               ♡ J7543
      ◊ Q73      W     E            ◊ J6
      ♣ AKJ         S               ♣ Q954
                  ♠ 87
                  ♡ AK96
                  ◊ AK95
                  ♣ 876
```

West	North	East	South
–	–	–	1NT
Pass	2♣	Pass	2♡
Pass	2NT	Pass	3NT
All Pass			

West led the king of clubs and continued with the ace and jack of the suit. East overtook with the queen and cashed the nine. Declarer threw a diamond and West had to find a discard. It looks all too obvious to throw a spade, but this West tried the effect of a small heart. East got off play with the jack of diamonds and declarer had to come up with a plan. He had eight tricks on top and it looked as if his best chance for a ninth was a squeeze, but which squeeze? It looked to him as if West had length in both red suits, so he cashed the ace and king of diamonds and then played three rounds of spades throwing a diamond from hand. Had West started with five hearts and three diamonds he would have been squeezed. As it was neither hand was under any pressure at all.

Had West discarded a spade, which happened at many other tables, declarer would probably have opted for a spade/diamond squeeze. He would have cashed the ace and king of diamonds followed by three rounds of hearts, which would have left West without resource.

East/West Game. Dealer East.

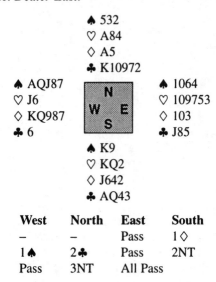

$\spadesuit$ 532
$\heartsuit$ A84
$\diamondsuit$ A5
$\clubsuit$ K10972

$\spadesuit$ AQJ87
$\heartsuit$ J6
$\diamondsuit$ KQ987
$\clubsuit$ 6

$\spadesuit$ 1064
$\heartsuit$ 109753
$\diamondsuit$ 103
$\clubsuit$ J85

$\spadesuit$ K9
$\heartsuit$ KQ2
$\diamondsuit$ J642
$\clubsuit$ AQ43

West	North	East	South
–	–	Pass	1 $\diamondsuit$
1 $\spadesuit$	2 $\clubsuit$	Pass	2NT
Pass	3NT	All Pass	

This deal occurred in the 1993 European Pairs and West opted for the jack of hearts lead, trying to be as passive as possible. Declarer won in hand and cashed his club and heart winners. West discarded, in order, the eight of diamonds, eight of spades, seven of spades, queen of spades and seven of diamonds (East discarded the ten of hearts and four of spades). When declarer cashed the ace of diamonds, West smoothly played the queen. Declarer thought West had come down to the singleton king of diamonds and so ducked a diamond to East's ten. A spade through now held declarer to nine tricks. This won the prize for the Best Defended Hand for Brian Senior.

3. A losing option

One of the most basic ways to give declarer a losing option is to playing the card we are known to hold. Suppose the layout of the heart suit is:

$\heartsuit$ AJ5

$\heartsuit$ Q106 $\heartsuit$ 842

$\heartsuit$ K973

Declarer plays a heart to his jack, which holds, placing West with the queen. He now cashes the ace. If we play the ten he knows we have the queen and will always play the king on the next round. However, if we drop the queen, he may well think partner has 10842 and finesse the nine on the next round.

Similarly, suppose declarer is playing a side suit of AQxxx in dummy facing a singleton in hand. If he plays to dummy's queen which holds and then ruffs one, unless we can think of a good reason to do otherwise we should play the king as early as possible. Until we play it he knows it is safe for him to ruff low; as soon as we have played the king he can no longer be sure.

Here are some more examples:

$$\heartsuit\ 1084$$
$$\heartsuit\ K76 \qquad\qquad \heartsuit\ J9$$
$$\heartsuit\ AQ532$$

Assuming declarer needs four tricks in this suit he will play low to his queen and later cash the ace, dropping the jack. However, if we play the jack on the first round of the suit, he may well play low to his eight next time, playing West for K976.

$$\heartsuit\ AJ83$$
$$\heartsuit\ K2 \qquad\qquad \heartsuit\ 1096$$
$$\heartsuit\ Q754$$

Declarer will probably start with a small card to dummy's jack. If, as East, we play low, his only chance of making four tricks will be to cash the ace dropping partner's king. If, on the other hand, we play the nine or ten he may cross back to hand and run the queen, playing us for ten-nine doubleton.

$$\heartsuit\ KQ94$$
$$\heartsuit\ 10863 \qquad\qquad \heartsuit\ A$$
$$\heartsuit\ J752$$

Declarer will no doubt start with a heart to dummy's queen and East's ace. If as West we play low to this trick, declarer will later cash his jack and finesse through our ten – he cannot pick up the suit when East has four cards. However, if we play the eight he may play the queen next, as he may place East with A1063.

These positions do not only arise when declarer broaches the suit. Suppose we are defending against a no trump contract and the suit layout is:

$$\heartsuit\ K54$$
$$\heartsuit\ QJ92 \qquad\qquad \heartsuit\ A86$$
$$\heartsuit\ 1073$$

If we switch to the queen declarer will undoubtedly duck and run the next lead around to his ten, thus preventing the run of the suit. Now suppose the layout is:

$$\heartsuit\ K54$$
$$\heartsuit\ Q82 \qquad\qquad \heartsuit\ AJ96$$
$$\heartsuit\ 1073$$

Switching to the queen rather than a small card may well see declarer ducking and now we can run the whole suit. And even more interesting is:

$$\heartsuit\ K54$$
$$\heartsuit\ AQ2 \qquad\qquad \heartsuit\ J986$$
$$\heartsuit\ 1073$$

Switch to the queen, which will probably hold. When we follow with the two, declarer may well run this to partner's jack and thus make no tricks in the suit.

Have a look at this problem:

North/South Game. Dealer East.

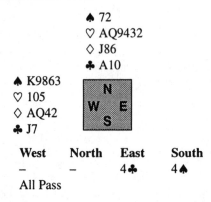

♠ 72
♡ AQ9432
◇ J86
♣ A10

♠ K9863
♡ 105
◇ AQ42
♣ J7

West	North	East	South
–	–	4♣	4♠
All Pass			

You lead the jack of clubs against South's four spades. Dummy wins with the ace as partner plays the six and declarer the queen. Declarer plays a spade from dummy to his queen, partner playing the four of clubs. Plan the defence.

Gather the evidence: It looks as if partner has eight clubs headed by the king. He has chosen to play very middling cards so should not have either red-suit king. You can see three defensive tricks but need to find a fourth.

Make a plan: As a matter of general principle you should duck the spade. No doubt declarer will continue with another spade which you will win. The only chance of two tricks seems to be in the diamond suit and that requires partner to hold the ten of diamonds.

Implement the plan: Play the two of diamonds. The full deal:

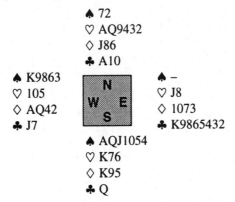

```
                    ♠ 72
                    ♡ AQ9432
                    ◊ J86
                    ♣ A10
   ♠ K9863                          ♠ –
   ♡ 105              N             ♡ J8
   ◊ AQ42          W     E          ◊ 1073
   ♣ J7               S             ♣ K9865432
                    ♠ AQJ1054
                    ♡ K76
                    ◊ K95
                    ♣ Q
```

This is the only switch to give declarer a problem. Should he play low, catering for you to have A10xx, or should he play the jack, which is right when you have AQxx? You have forced him to guess.

Game All. Dealer North.

```
                    ♠ AJ3
                    ♡ J97
                    ◊ AQJ3
                    ♣ 643
   ♠ Q10652                         ♠ K874
   ♡ Q54               N            ♡ 10863
   ◊ 98             W     E         ◊ 54
   ♣ 1087              S            ♣ AJ5
                    ♠ 9
                    ♡ AK2
                    ◊ K10762
                    ♣ KQ92
```

West	North	East	South
–	1NT	Pass	2NT(i)
Pass	3♣	Pass	3♠(ii)
Pass	3NT	Pass	4◊
Pass	4♠	Double	4NT
Pass	5♠	Pass	6◊
All Pass			

(i) Diamonds
(ii) Shortage

This hand, from the 1995 Lederer Memorial Trophy, won a Best Defended Hand award for Turkey's Nafiz Zorlu. West led a heart and the jack won in dummy. Declarer, Ireland's Hugh McGann, drew trumps eliminating hearts and spades along the way. He then played a club from the dummy and East played the jack, thus giving declarer a losing option in the suit. Declarer duly crossed to dummy and played a club to the nine, one down.

At first glance, declarer's play looks foolish, for who would play the jack of clubs from jack-ten? But, if declarer's clubs were AQ8x, it would be necessary in order to prevent partner being endplayed.

As well as trying to give declarer a losing option as often as possible, we should try to remove *partner's* losing options. This example hand was given by Jeff Rubens in his Bols Bridge Tip, 'Honour Thy Partner'.

Game All. Dealer South.

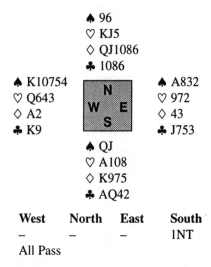

| ♠ 96 |
| ♡ KJ5 |
| ◇ QJ1086 |
| ♣ 1086 |

♠ K10754		♠ A832
♡ Q643		♡ 972
◇ A2		◇ 43
♣ K9		♣ J753

| ♠ QJ |
| ♡ A108 |
| ◇ K975 |
| ♣ AQ42 |

West	North	East	South
–	–	–	1NT
All Pass			

West led the five of spades to the six, ace and jack. East returned the two of spades to the queen, king and nine. West can see seven tricks for the defence: five spades, one diamond and one club. But unless East leads a club early in the play South will strike first with two hearts, four diamonds and a club. The average West, having reasoned this far, leads the spade four at the third trick. But East may win and unthinkingly return a spade. A good defender plays the seven of spades before leading the four. When East wins he is out of spades and has no alternative to the winning club switch.

6
MASTERCLASS

This chapter is a compendium of wonderful hands. It is for you to read and enjoy rather than study in detail. It shows the experts at their best. Some of the hands are very complicated, some fairly straightforward, but in each case the expert's play is logical, based on analytical deduction.

The first deal features the Hackett brothers, both Junior World Champions, who picked up 13 IMPs on this deal when their teammates made 3NT and they beat the same contract by five tricks.

Love All. Dealer West.

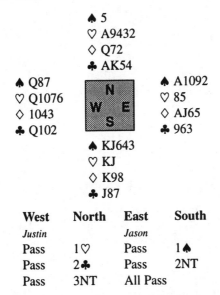

```
                    ♠ 5
                    ♡ A9432
                    ♦ Q72
                    ♣ AK54
    ♠ Q87                          ♠ A1092
    ♡ Q1076          N             ♡ 85
    ♦ 1043       W       E         ♦ AJ65
    ♣ Q102           S             ♣ 963
                    ♠ KJ643
                    ♡ KJ
                    ♦ K98
                    ♣ J87
```

West	North	East	South
Justin		*Jason*	
Pass	1♡	Pass	1♠
Pass	2♣	Pass	2NT
Pass	3NT	All Pass	

At the other table, Paul Hackett, father of Jason and Justin, was the declarer in three no trumps. He got a club lead that ran to his jack. He cashed the king of hearts, then led the jack of hearts, covered and ducked.

West switched to the ten of diamonds which went to the queen and ace, and declarer finessed the nine of diamonds successfully on the return. He then led a club to the king, cashed the ace of hearts and led another heart to set up the long card in the suit. Now he had nine tricks – three hearts, four clubs and two diamonds.

Justin also led a club, the *ten*, and declarer again let it ride to his jack. He followed with the eight of clubs to the queen, king and six, and took a losing heart finesse. Justin returned the two of clubs and declarer, playing the opening lead to be from Q1092, finessed, losing to the nine. A spade went to the jack and queen, and the heart return was won with South's king. Now the king of diamonds was allowed to hold, but the next diamond went to the queen and ace. After cashing the jack and five of diamonds, Jason led the nine of spades, ducked, the ten of spades, ducked, and the ace of spades. That was nine tricks for the defence – four spades, one club, three diamonds and a heart.

North/South Game. Dealer West.

♠ AQ75
♡ AQ74
◇ 10982
♣ 8

♠ 96   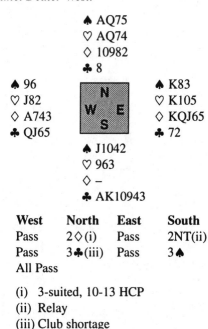   ♠ K83
♡ J82   ♡ K105
◇ A743   ◇ KQJ65
♣ QJ65   ♣ 72

♠ J1042
♡ 963
◇ –
♣ AK10943

West	North	East	South
Pass	2◇(i)	Pass	2NT(ii)
Pass	3♣(iii)	Pass	3♠
All Pass			

(i)   3-suited, 10-13 HCP
(ii) Relay
(iii) Club shortage

It is usually right to lead a trump when one of the opponents has shown a three-suited hand and this was no exception. West led the six of spades to his partner's king and East continued with a spade to dummy's ace. Declarer played the ace and king of clubs and ruffed a club with dummy's seven of spades. This was the moment of truth. Had East overruffed and returned, say, a diamond, declarer would have ruffed, ruffed another club, ruffed a diamond and claimed nine tricks.

At the table East declined to ruff and declarer had no answer. He ruffed a diamond to hand but if he had ruffed a fourth club, another diamond ruff would have exhausted him of trumps. His best chance was the heart finesse. When it lost East was quick to play his last trump and declarer was two down.

Game All. Dealer East.

```
                    ♠ 974
                    ♡ AK
                    ◇ A9432
                    ♣ Q83
  ♠ KQJ6                              ♠ 5
  ♡ 94                                ♡ 108632
  ◇ QJ6                               ◇ 107
  ♣ K964                              ♣ AJ1075
                    ♠ A10832
                    ♡ QJ75
                    ◇ K85
                    ♣ 2
```

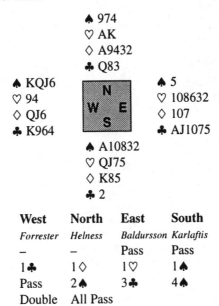

West	North	East	South
Forrester	Helness	Baldursson	Karlaftis
–	–	Pass	Pass
1♣	1◇	1♡	1♠
Pass	2♠	3♣	4♠
Double	All Pass		

Against South's poor four spade contract, West led the four of clubs to East's ten. East returned a club which declarer ruffed. Now the ace and king of hearts and another club ruff were followed by the diamond ace and king and the queen of hearts which West ruffed high. This was the position:

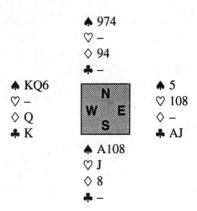

```
              ♠ 974
              ♡ –
              ◇ 94
              ♣ –
♠ KQ6                      ♠ 5
♡ –           ┌─────┐      ♡ 108
◇ Q           │  N  │      ◇ –
♣ K           │W   E│      ♣ AJ
              │  S  │
              └─────┘
              ♠ A108
              ♡ J
              ◇ 8
              ♣ –
```

West now led the queen of diamonds, Had this held he would have played a club which declarer would have ruffed in the dummy and played a spade to his ten, endplaying West, and getting out for one down. However, East had a better idea. He ruffed his partner's queen of diamonds and led another heart. Thus West scored another ruff and could get off play with the king of clubs, sitting back to wait for another trump trick.

Love All. Dealer South.

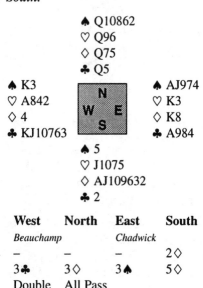

```
              ♠ Q10862
              ♡ Q96
              ◇ Q75
              ♣ Q5
♠ K3                       ♠ AJ974
♡ A842        ┌─────┐      ♡ K3
◇ 4           │  N  │      ◇ K8
♣ KJ10763     │W   E│      ♣ A984
              │  S  │
              └─────┘
              ♠ 5
              ♡ J1075
              ◇ AJ109632
              ♣ 2
```

West	North	East	South
Beauchamp		*Chadwick*	
–	–	–	2◇
3♣	3◇	3♠	5◇
Double	All Pass		

This deal comes from the final of the 1995 Grand National Australian Open Teams in which the winning team earns the right to represent their zone in the Bermuda Bowl.

South's bidding was eccentric. He had too much playing strength for a weak two on the first round but then masterminded the auction later on by bidding on when not invited to do so. Still, he had ended up in a reasonable spot as it looks as if six clubs is cold for his opponents so they needed to take as many tricks in defence as possible.

West led the king of spades and East played a suit-preference nine. Now the two of hearts went to the king, a heart was returned to West's ace and the four of hearts was led for East to ruff. Now a club went to West's king and a fourth heart was ruffed with the king of diamonds. The maximum 800 penalty had been achieved.

Love All. Dealer East.

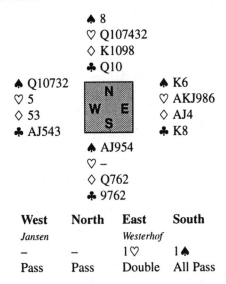

```
                    ♠ 8
                    ♡ Q107432
                    ♦ K1098
                    ♣ Q10
     ♠ Q10732                      ♠ K6
     ♡ 5              N            ♡ AKJ986
     ♦ 53          W   E          ♦ AJ4
     ♣ AJ543          S            ♣ K8
                    ♠ AJ954
                    ♡ –
                    ♦ Q762
                    ♣ 9762
```

West	North	East	South
Jansen		*Westerhof*	
–	–	1♡	1♠
Pass	Pass	Double	All Pass

This deal was played in the lowly contract of one spade doubled at many tables in the 1995 European Championships in Vilamoura. There are many ways to hold declarer to four tricks. One of the most attractive was found by Piet Jansen and Jan Westerhof of the Netherlands.

West led his singleton heart and declarer ruffed. With nothing else to do, declarer tried a diamond to the king and ace. East, who had a somewhat better trump holding than his partner was likely to expect, switched to the king of spades. Declarer won the ace of spades, cashed the queen of diamonds and played another diamond, West discarding a club. East won his jack of diamonds, cashed the king of clubs and played the king of hearts. Declarer discarded a club but West, anxious to avoid a possible trump endplay, ruffed. He then played the ace of clubs. When he cashed his jack of clubs, this was the position:

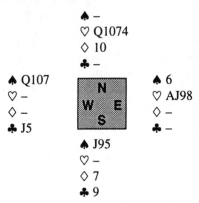

```
                    ♠ –
                    ♡ Q1074
                    ◇ 10
                    ♣ –
     ♠ Q107      ┌─────────┐    ♠ 6
     ♡ –         │    N    │    ♡ AJ98
     ◇ –         │  W   E  │    ◇ –
     ♣ J5        │    S    │    ♣ –
                 └─────────┘
                    ♠ J95
                    ♡ –
                    ◇ 7
                    ♣ 9
```

The defenders want to restrict declarer to one more trick. If West is allowed to win his jack of clubs the defenders are in trouble. Say West plays another club, declarer will ruff and play a diamond; West will have to ruff this trick with the seven (had he preserved a small trump East could have overruffed with the six) and will then be endplayed in trumps.

Foreseeing this, East ruffed his partner's club winner and played a heart. There was nothing declarer could do. If he ruffed, West would overruff, cash his queen of trumps and play a master club. So declarer discarded a diamond. It did not matter now. West could have discarded his club, overruffed the next heart and cashed the queen of trumps – declarer would just have made one trump. However, West preferred to enter into the spirit of the situation: he ruffed his partner's heart winner, exited with a club and made the last two tricks with his queen and ten of trumps.

It may not have been one of the best defences of the tournament but it does illustrate both partners trying their hardest to avoid endplaying the other.

Game All. Dealer East.

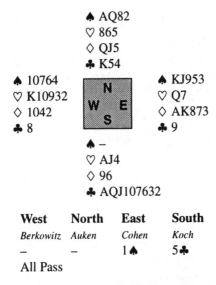

```
                    ♠ AQ82
                    ♡ 865
                    ◊ QJ5
                    ♣ K54
   ♠ 10764          ┌─────────┐    ♠ KJ953
   ♡ K10932         │    N    │    ♡ Q7
   ◊ 1042           │ W     E │    ◊ AK873
   ♣ 8              │    S    │    ♣ 9
                    └─────────┘
                    ♠ –
                    ♡ AJ4
                    ◊ 96
                    ♣ AQJ107632
```

West	North	East	South
Berkowitz	*Auken*	*Cohen*	*Koch*
–	–	1♠	5♣
All Pass			

This deal comes from the Politiken World Pairs Tournament in Copenhagen in 1995 and illustrates an excellent co-operative defence from David Berkowitz and Larry Cohen.

West led the four of spades against five clubs. Declarer won with the ace, discarding a diamond, and played a low diamond from the dummy. East thought long and hard about this but eventually played small. West won with his ten and played a second spade, ruffed high by declarer. Now the club seven to the king and a high diamond ruff, the club three to the four and a high diamond ruff. Declarer cashed the ace of hearts and East smoothly unblocked his queen. Declarer played a small heart and the spotlight fell on West. Was this an example of the Crocodile Coup (page 97)? Did partner hold ♡QJ when it was essential for West to play the king? Or did he hold a small heart when to play the king of hearts would be a serious error? David Berkowitz completed an excellent defence by his side when he played the nine. Now there was a second heart trick to beat the game.

There is a logical reason for West to play the nine on the second heart but it does assume that his partner is capable of lightning analysis of a very complex position. Had East held ♡QJ he should have played the jack. Why? Because then East could work out the position because with AQx declarer would have taken a simple heart finesse through the opening bidder.

Love All. Dealer North.

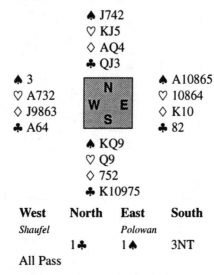

```
                  ♠ J742
                  ♡ KJ5
                  ♢ AQ4
                  ♣ QJ3
    ♠ 3                        ♠ A10865
    ♡ A732                     ♡ 10864
    ♢ J9863                    ♢ K10
    ♣ A64                      ♣ 82
                  ♠ KQ9
                  ♡ Q9
                  ♢ 752
                  ♣ K10975
```

West	North	East	South
Shaufel		*Polowan*	
	1♣	1♠	3NT
All Pass			

This deal was a contender for the Best Defended Hand of 1994. It features Israeli's Eliakim Shaufel playing with Michael Polowan of the USA.

West started by leading the six of diamonds. Declarer won with the ace and East dropped the king! It was fairly clear that partner had the diamond jack, so the king and ten were equals. When declarer knocked out the ace of clubs West continued with the jack of diamonds, squashing his partner's ten, and then could clear the suit. A good combined effort.

North/South Game. Dealer South.

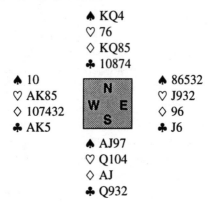

```
                  ♠ KQ4
                  ♡ 76
                  ♢ KQ85
                  ♣ 10874
    ♠ 10                       ♠ 86532
    ♡ AK85                     ♡ J932
    ♢ 107432                   ♢ 96
    ♣ AK5                      ♣ J6
                  ♠ AJ97
                  ♡ Q104
                  ♢ AJ
                  ♣ Q932
```

West	North	East	South
–	–	–	1NT(i)
Pass	3NT	All Pass	

(i)   14-16

On this deal it looks as though declarer should make nine tricks in his no trump game with no problems. He has eight tricks on top and with the jacks of hearts and clubs well placed it is hard to see how the defence can prevail. This deal occurred in the 1994 Junior European Championship on VuGraph and the Danish North/South had stopped in three clubs in the other room. The VuGraph commentators had predicted a swing to Sweden.

Jacob Røn of Denmark led the ace of hearts and, after considerable thought, switched to the ten of spades. As the cards lie, declarer could have won in dummy and played a heart, but if West had had another spade to play, the contract would have been scuppered. Instead, declarer fell into a worse trap. He won the spade in dummy, unblocked his diamonds, crossed to a spade and cashed the king of diamonds. The contract was now unmakeable.

Declarer should have realised the problems he was going to run into and played a club at trick three, thus untangling his communication problems.

Love All. Dealer South.

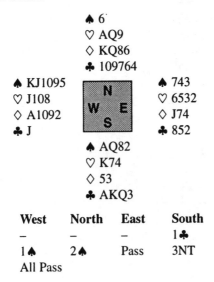

```
              ♠ 6
              ♡ AQ9
              ◊ KQ86
              ♣ 109764
♠ KJ1095                    ♠ 743
♡ J108          N           ♡ 6532
◊ A1092      W     E         ◊ J74
♣ J             S           ♣ 852
              ♠ AQ82
              ♡ K74
              ◊ 53
              ♣ AKQ3
```

West	North	East	South
–	–	–	1♣
1♠	2♠	Pass	3NT
All Pass			

This deal cropped in a pairs qualifying session at an American National. Most declarers made twelve tricks in no trumps but a few Wests (including Bobby Levin, former world champion and many-times North American champion) found the right defence.

The opening lead was the jack of hearts. Declarer won in hand and played a diamond to the king. Now a club back to hand and another diamond. The winning defence was to duck this as well. Now declarer rattled off his winners in hearts and clubs, arriving at this position:

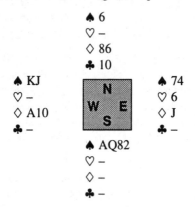

On the ten of clubs West was able to discard the ace of diamonds, leaving declarer with only eleven tricks. Had West risen with the ace of diamonds earlier in the play he would have been squeezed on this trick with no discard that would prevent declarer from taking twelve tricks.

Love All. Dealer South.

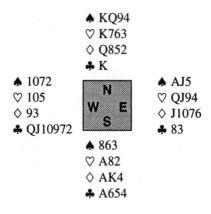

West	North	East	South
–	–	–	1NT
Pass	2♣	Pass	2◊
Pass	3NT	All Pass	

This hand won the Best Defended Hand of the Year in 1992 for America's Mike Passell, who was East.

West led the queen of clubs to dummy's king. Declarer played a diamond to his king and a spade to dummy's king ... Passell played the jack! Declarer now crossed back to hand and played a spade to the queen, catering for singleton jack or jack-ten doubleton with East. Passell won the ace of spades, cleared the clubs, and the ten of spades became an entry to the long clubs before declarer had established his two spade tricks.

There are plenty of defensive possibilities when declarer has KQ9x facing xxx. This defence bears some resemblance to the one described on page 131.

Game All. Dealer East.

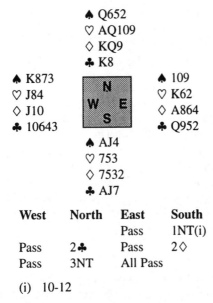

```
                    ♠ Q652
                    ♡ AQ109
                    ◊ KQ9
                    ♣ K8
    ♠ K873                      ♠ 109
    ♡ J84            N          ♡ K62
    ◊ J10        W     E        ◊ A864
    ♣ 10643         S           ♣ Q952
                    ♠ AJ4
                    ♡ 753
                    ◊ 7532
                    ♣ AJ7
```

West	North	East	South
		Pass	1NT(i)
Pass	2♣	Pass	2◊
Pass	3NT	All Pass	

(i) 10-12

This deal turned up in a Danish invitational event and features Matthias Bruun, one of the strong Danish juniors. West led the three of spades to the nine and declarer's jack. Declarer played a heart to dummy's nine and

East ducked. Now a spade to the ace and a second heart to the ten which East also ducked! Declarer played the king of diamonds from dummy, also ducked. The queen of diamonds was won with the ace and another diamond played to dummy's nine. Now the king of clubs and a club to the ace gave declarer eight tricks. He could have played safe for his contract by cashing the ace of hearts, but ... convinced the king of hearts was with West, he played a heart to the queen and made no more tricks. One down.

With the recent demise of Terence Reese, there can be no more fitting epitaph than to include the following deceptive play that he made some sixty years ago while still a student at Oxford University.

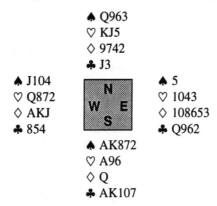

West led out two top diamonds against South's spade slam. Declarer ruffed the second and played the ace and king of clubs and ruffed a club. It was clear to Reese, East, that declarer would be able to ruff a second club in the dummy, he tried the effect of dropping the queen of clubs. Declarer continued with the queen and ace of spades. When East showed out on the second round it seemed safe to play the master ten of clubs, discarding a heart from dummy. Then declarer could ruff a heart in dummy rather than rely on the heart finesse. A rather surprised West made his jack of trumps to defeat the slam.

-o-o-o-o-o-o-

Of course, as defenders in this book we have relied on declarer playing a simple game with little of the deception that is possible, and we have by and large had straightforward evidence. In real life declarers do play a deceptive game, partner is not always awake or has a mind of his o wn, and the evidence is often contradictory. How we sort that out is another story...